LIGHT

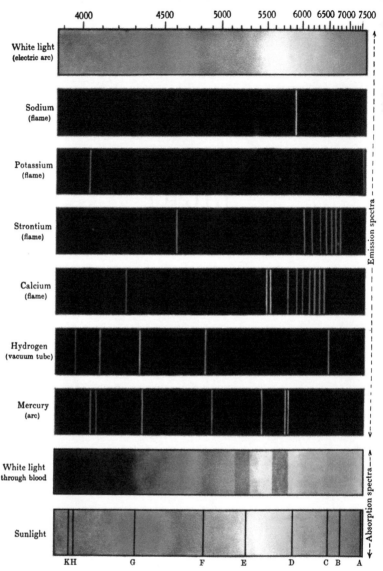

The top seven spectra are emission spectra and the bottom two are absorption spectra. Note the two dark bands in the absorption spectrum of a dilute blood solution—a delicate blood test. The spectrum of sunlight is crossed by hundreds of dark lines and only the most prominent ones are marked. A and B are due to absorption by oxygen in the earth's atmosphere, and the rest by the vapours surrounding the sun; e.g. C and F by hydrogen, and D by sodium vapour. Note also that these dark lines are in the same position as the corresponding bright lines in the spectra of hydrogen and sodium.

The scale at the top represents wave-lengths in Ångström units (1 unit $= 10^{-8}$ cm.).

LIGHT

by

A. E. E. McKENZIE, M.A.

Trinity College, Cambridge
Assistant Master at Repton School

"These principles I consider as general Laws of Nature;
their Truth appearing to us by *Phaenomena*, though their
Causes be not yet discovered."

SIR ISAAC NEWTON: *Optics*

CAMBRIDGE

AT THE UNIVERSITY PRESS

1936

CAMBRIDGE
UNIVERSITY PRESS

University Printing House, Cambridge CB2 8BS, United Kingdom

Cambridge University Press is part of the University of Cambridge.

It furthers the University's mission by disseminating knowledge in the pursuit of education, learning and research at the highest international levels of excellence.

www.cambridge.org
Information on this title: www.cambridge.org/9781107452541

© Cambridge University Press 1936

First published 1936
First paperback edition 2014

A catalogue record for this publication is available from the British Library

ISBN 978-1-107-45254-1 Paperback

CONTENTS

LIGHT

PREFACE

This volume, following my *Hydrostatics and Mechanics* and *Heat*, is the third of a series of Physics text-books of School Certificate and 1st M.B. standard.

While dealing mainly with geometrical optics, I have touched upon the wave and corpuscular (or quantum) theories, and given a brief mention of the explanations offered by each of the various phenomena.

I have adopted the recommendations in the Report of the Physical Society on "The Teaching of Geometrical Optics" with respect to sign conventions—"Among practical workers in optics it has long been the predominant custom to call a converging lens positive and a diverging lens negative. This convention is now universal among opticians. We strongly and unanimously recommend that this sign convention regarding lenses and mirrors, universally employed among practical opticians, should also be followed by the teaching profession."

Two alternative conventions, both taking the focal length of a converging lens as positive, were recommended in the Report. After practical experience in teaching both, I have decided to adopt the second: distances actually travelled by the light are taken as positive and distances along a virtual ray as negative. Boys do not seem to find any more difficulty with this convention than with one based on position in a Cartesian system. Its superiority lies chiefly in its elegance. The distance of a real object from a lens or mirror is taken as positive instead of negative; in the case of a real image formed by a concave mirror, u, v, f are all positive instead of negative; and one formula, $\frac{1}{u} + \frac{1}{v} = \frac{1}{f}$ applies to both lenses and spherical mirrors.

I am encouraged in my decision to adopt the second, alternative, convention by the enthusiastic and almost unanimous support it evoked at the discussion on sign conventions during the annual meeting of the Science Masters' Association in January 1936.

Although I have preferred to treat lenses before spherical mirrors, there is no reason why, using this convention, the order should not be reversed.

The terms "converging" and "diverging", as applied to lenses, have been used in preference to "convex" and "concave".

Many optical phenomena can be recorded by the camera, and the photographs, in this book, of beams being reflected and refracted, of images in mirrors, caustics, and no-parallax adjustments, were taken by Mr D. G. A. Dyson of King Edward VI School, Stratford-on-Avon, to whom I am under a deep obligation. Mr Dyson has also accomplished the more difficult task of photographing water waves to demonstrate interference, diffraction, reflection at plane and curved surfaces, and refraction both at a plane surface and through a lens.

I am under a further obligation to Mr Dyson for reading the manuscript, and making numerous important suggestions. To him, for example, I am indebted for the photometry experiments with a photo-electric cell. Fig. 120 is a copy of light distribution curves he obtained by a modification of a method designed by the General Electric Research Laboratories.

My colleague, Mr R. E. Williams, has read the manuscript and I am grateful to him for his valuable criticisms.

The photographs of light passing through lenses in a smoke box, the "fish's-eye" view, multiple reflections of a candle flame, and the luminous jet, were taken for me by Mr B. F. Brown in the Repton Laboratories. I must also express my thanks to Mr H. Gresley, of the Art School, Repton, for painting the continuous and two absorption spectra for the Frontispiece.

Messrs Zeiss very kindly sent to Germany for blocks to illustrate the manufacture of lenses. The photographs of the mirror, etc. of the 100 in. reflector were obtained from Mount Wilson and those of the Yerkes telescope and the eclipse of the moon from the University of Chicago.

Prof. A. O. Rankine very kindly loaned me a negative of the photograph of the mirage which he took in Persia.

I am grateful to my pupils, Mr G. S. Dawes and Mr G. A. Vickers, who have worked out the answers to the examples.

Finally I must express my thanks to the following Examining Bodies for permission to reproduce School Certificate questions: the Oxford and Cambridge Joint Board (O. & C.), the Northern University Joint Matriculation Board (N.), the University of London (L.), the Cambridge Local (C.), and Oxford Local (O.), Examination Syndicates. The letters in brackets will be found printed after the questions to designate their source.

A. E. E. M.

Repton
June 1936

LIST OF PLATES

LIGHT

Chapter I

THE PROPAGATION OF LIGHT

In order that an object may be seen, there must pass from it into the eye something which we call *light*. In a perfectly dark room there is no light and objects are invisible: if the eyes are shut, no light can enter them and nothing can be seen.

An electric lamp emits its own light and is said to be *luminous*. Other objects near to the lamp can be seen although they emit no light of their own. They are said to be *illuminated*. Light from the lamp falls upon them and then proceeds to the eye, thus rendering them visible.

What is light?

Light is a form of energy. It is generated, for instance, in an electric lamp, by the transformation of electrical energy into light energy. The light energy can be converted back into electrical energy by allowing it to fall on a photo-electric cell.

The energy reaching the earth from the sun (without which the earth would quickly become cold and lifeless) arrives in the form of light and other invisible radiation similar to light.

But what is the actual form of light energy? Cannot a definite picture be given?

There are two historic theories of light, neither of which, after 300 years of rivalry, is yet completely predominant. Until recently it seemed that one of these theories, after overshadowing the other for more than a century, had been utterly discredited. But now once more, in a modified form, it has been revived to explain certain phenomena.

The corpuscular theory.

This theory, known as the Corpuscular or Emission Theory, was developed largely by Sir Isaac Newton (1642–1727). He assumed that light consists of a stream of tiny moving particles,

M^cK

or corpuscles, which are shot out by a source of light, and which, on entering the eye and striking the retina, produce the sensation of sight.

The wave theory.

At about the same time a Dutch scientist, Christiaan Huygens (1629–95), put forward the theory that light, like sound, consists of some form of wave motion. When a stone is thrown into a lake, circular ripples or waves spread out from the spot where the stone entered the water. When a pistol is fired, sound waves in the air spread out from the pistol and cause the ear drums to vibrate. But since light travels through a vacuum and waves cannot exist without some form of medium, Huygens had to postulate that space is filled with an invisible and completely undetected medium called the aether.

Interference.

Newton's prestige was so great that little attention was paid to the wave theory until the beginning of the nineteenth century (and strangely enough no notice was taken of the fact that Newton did believe that waves were partly responsible for the propagation of light). At that time certain phenomena were discovered which the corpuscular theory was powerless to explain, but which could be accounted for very neatly and convincingly on the wave theory. Briefly, it was discovered that, under certain conditions, two rays of light could be made to annihilate one another and produce darkness. The phenomenon is called *interference*. Fig. 1 is a photograph of interference bands obtained by dividing a beam of light into two,

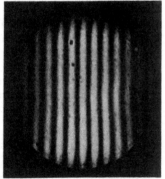

D. G. A. Dyson

Fig. 1. Interference bands: produced by Young's method, using blue light.

(making two virtual sources), and shining the two parts on to a screen. This experiment was first performed by Dr Thomas Young. We shall not enter into details of his experimental arrangements, but merely assert the fact which he discovered, namely, that two beams of light produce dark bands.

The explanation, on the wave theory, of dark interference bands is that two waves happen so to fit that the crests of one occupy the same position in the aether as the troughs of the other, with the result that they annul each other (see Fig. 2).

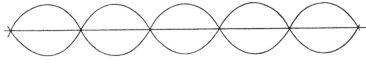

Fig. 2

Interference between two sets of water waves can be demonstrated by means of a ripple tank. This consists of a large shallow tank with a glass bottom, containing water, under which is a powerful arc light. Two trains of circular waves may be set up by allowing a steel ruler, clamped to the side of the tank and carrying two wire prongs which just dip into the water, to vibrate.

Plate I (a), facing p. 32, is a photograph of interference bands (the radial, spoke-like bands) produced in this way. Fig. 3 illustrates how the bands are formed. S_1 and S_2 are the two sources of the circular waves. The continuous semicircles represent crests and the dotted semicircles troughs. Where a crest and a trough coincide, marked × in the figure, the water is quiescent: where two crests or two troughs coincide, marked o, the waves are doubly large.

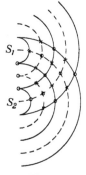

Fig. 3

The photograph in Fig. 1 represents a cross-section of these bands parallel to the line joining the sources of light.

Although the detailed study of interference is beyond the scope of this book, we mention it here because of its decisive influence in establishing the wave theory. Allied to it is what we might call the phenomenon of non-interference. For two sets of waves can pass through each other and though they produce interference bands where they cross, they emerge unchanged. This explains why, when a beam of white light is passed through a beam of red light, the white light emerges uncoloured. It is difficult to explain on the corpuscular theory how this can happen. Indeed, one of the early criticisms of the corpuscular theory was that if it were true, it would be impossible to look a man in the eye. For the light corpuscles from his eye would collide with the light corpuscles from one's own.

The photo-electric effect.

During the nineteenth century the wave theory was used to explain all the known facts about light, and the corpuscular theory was discarded. "Every new discovery fitted perfectly into the scheme which the theory prepared for it." But at the beginning of the twentieth century further facts were discovered which are difficult to explain on the wave theory. The energy of a source of light appears to be emitted, not in the form of a continuous stream, but in little bundles or corpuscles of energy called *photons*.

When light falls upon certain metals it causes the emission of tiny particles of negative electricity, called *electrons*. This is known as the *photo-electric effect*. Now the velocity with which these electrons are ejected does not depend, as might certainly be expected, on the intensity of the light, nor does it vary appreciably with different metals. However weak the light which falls upon the metal, the velocity of the electrons is the same. There seems no escape from the conclusion that the energy of the light is contained in the form of small corpuscles or photons, and that an electron is ejected from an atom when a photon happens to strike and be absorbed by it.

The inadequacy of the wave theory to explain this phenomenon is brought out strikingly by Sir William Bragg in the following analogy: "Suppose we drop a plank into the sea from a given height, say 100 ft.; there is a splash, and waves spread away over the surface of the water. They pass by boats and ships without any effect and then after travelling thousands of miles they find a ship on which their effect is disastrous: a plank is torn out of the ship's side and hurled ninety feet into the air, or fifty feet, or twenty, all such numbers seem equally ridiculous. Yet this is a fair parallel to any explanation of the photo-electric effect on the simple wave theory."

In order to explain both interference and the photo-electric effect, it would seem that some combination of the wave and corpuscular theories is necessary. This is one of the most interesting problems of physics at the present time.

We shall, throughout our study of light, consider the explanations offered by both theories of the various phenomena.

Light travels in straight lines.

Since we can see an object only when light from it enters the eye, the fact that we cannot see round obstacles suggests that light travels in straight lines, a phenomenon called the Rectilinear Propagation of Light.

Light, therefore, may conveniently be represented by straight lines (called *rays*). A collection of rays is called a *beam* or a *pencil*.

Scattering of light.

In order to test whether light travels in straight lines it would seem that one need only produce a narrow beam of light, look at it, and observe whether it is straight. The sharp straight edges of a beam from a searchlight or a cinematograph projector are a matter of common observation. When we view such a beam from the side, however, none of its light could possibly enter the eye (assuming that light does travel in straight lines) unless some of the rays were deflected sideways. Such deflection, or *scattering* as it is called, is caused by rays striking particles of dust in the air. A beam from a lantern can be rendered more clearly visible by shaking chalk dust in its path. Further, it can be shown experimentally that if a beam of light is passed through a perfectly dustless space it is invisible when viewed from the side.

Twilight in a cloudless sky is caused by the scattering of light. After the sun has set below the horizon, complete and immediate darkness would result were it not for the fact that rays of sunlight passing above the earth's surface are deflected downwards by small particles in the atmosphere.

The pinhole camera.

A convincing proof that light travels in straight lines is the action of the pinhole camera.

This consists of a rectangular light-proof box with a pinhole (usually pierced in thin metal) in the middle of one face and a shutter arrangement to open and close the hole. Opposite the pinhole inside the box is placed a photographic plate.

The action of the camera can be demonstrated as follows. Place a lighted candle in front of a pinhole in a sheet of cardboard, and then place a screen behind the pinhole. A clear inverted image of the flame will be seen on the screen (see Fig. 4). A lighted candle is used as the object since it is giving out plenty of light and will therefore produce a bright image.

Now the top of the flame is sending out rays of light in all directions. Only a very narrow beam, however, passes through the pinhole and makes a small illuminated patch on the screen. Similarly a narrow beam from the bottom of the object B causes an illuminated patch at B'. From every point on the object a narrow beam of light passes through the pinhole, forming patches on the screen with the result that a complete image $A'B'$ is produced.

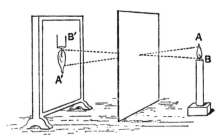

Fig. 4

If the hole is made too large each point on the object will cause a large patch on the screen: there will then be considerable overlapping of the patches and the image will be blurred. The smaller the hole, the sharper will be the image. However, if the hole is made very small, very little light will pass through it and the image will be dim. This would mean a long exposure in the actual camera. It is found also that if the diameter of the hole is decreased to less than about $\frac{1}{10}$ mm. in diameter (depending on the distance of the plate), the image, instead of becoming sharper, tends to become more blurred. On passing through these very tiny holes, the light, instead of continuing straight, spreads very slightly. The phenomenon, known as diffraction, is capable of explanation on the wave theory.

The shape of the hole has no appreciable effect on the definition of the image—why?

The image remains sharp when the distance between the screen and the pinhole is increased, but it is thereby enlarged and its brightness diminished. Also, objects at all distances from the pinhole give rise to sharp images on the screen.

The pinhole camera is not widely used. Its chief drawback is the long exposure required owing to the small amount of light which can pass through the pinhole. Its chief advantages are its cheapness and its wide field of view unaccompanied by distortion.

Fig. 5

The eye of a primitive creature called *Nautilus* works on the principle of the pinhole camera (see Fig. 5). A small hole takes the place of the lens to be found in the eyes of advanced living creatures.

Shadows.

The formation of sharp shadows is a further proof that light cannot bend round objects. But most shadows, including all those thrown by objects obstructing sunlight, are blurred. How are we to account for this?

Using a "point" source of light, such as a motor headlamp or a similar small filament lamp, a sharp shadow is thrown by an obstacle. If, however, an extended source of light, an ordinary pearl or opal lamp, is used a blurred shadow results (see Fig. 6). In the diagram AB represents the lamp and PQ the obstacle. The black part of the shadow is called the *umbra* (Latin—shade), and the shaded portion the *penumbra* (*paene*—nearly). The shadow on the screen, which is really a cross-section of the whole shadow, consists, if the obstacle is spherical, of a central black disc with fairly sharply defined circumference (the umbra) surrounded by a circular lighter band with a blurred outer circumference (the penumbra). The penumbra becomes gradually less dark towards its outer edge until eventually it ceases to be shadow at all.

It is clear from the diagram that no light from the source can penetrate the umbra. However, light from part of the source does illuminate the penumbra. Thus a point M in the penumbra receives light from all points between CB in the source but none from *CA*. On passing towards the outer rim of the penumbra rays from an increasingly greater area of the source can reach the screen, until eventually rays from the whole source reach it and the penumbra ends.

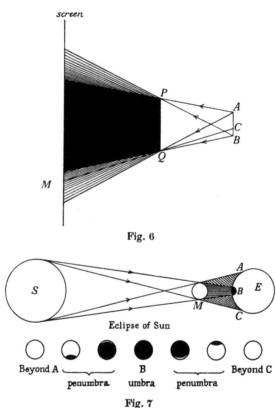

Fig. 6

Fig. 7

Eclipse of the sun.

At an eclipse a shadow of gigantic size is thrown by one of the heavenly bodies.

An *eclipse of the sun* is caused by the moon becoming interposed between the earth and the sun (see Fig. 7). At places on the earth's surface falling within the umbra the sun is completely covered by the moon and it is said to be totally eclipsed. At places within the penumbra the sun is not completely covered by the moon and here the eclipse is partial. The appearance of the sun from different places on the earth's surface which lie within the moon's shadow is shown in Fig. 7.

Since the earth is rotating and at the same time moving round the sun, and since also the moon is moving round the earth, the

By courtesy of the Royal Astronomical Society

Fig. 8. The solar corona, seen only at a total eclipse of the sun. It is a pearly white halo caused by very fine dust. Note also the prominences, vast tongues of flame much larger than the earth.

total phase of an eclipse cannot last for more than a few minutes at a particular place. Seven minutes is the longest possible time of totality.

At any instant during an eclipse the moon's shadow on the earth's surface is an oval patch (owing to the obliquity of the rays), but during the course of the eclipse this patch moves across the earth's surface tracing out a belt. The motion of the edge of this belt, like a black curtain sweeping over the earth, is a very impressive sight. A beautiful phenomenon which can be viewed only at a total eclipse is the corona, a pearly glow surrounding the sun, due probably to the lighting up of fine dust forced out for millions of miles from the sun's surface by the pressure of light. The prominences of the sun, vast tongues of crimson glowing vapours, can also be seen (Fig. 8).

Since the moon revolves round the earth once every 28 days, it might be expected that the sun would be eclipsed once each lunar month. The orbit of the moon round the earth, however, is slightly inclined (at 5°) to the orbit of the earth round the sun. Consequently the sun, moon and earth are only occasionally in line.

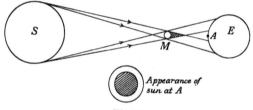

Fig. 9

The path of the moon round the earth is a slightly elongated circle called an ellipse, and the distance of the moon from the earth therefore varies. Usually at an eclipse the moon is at such a distance from the earth that the latter just falls within the umbra. The apparent size of the moon is then slightly greater than the apparent size of the sun. It occasionally happens that the earth is beyond the umbra. The apparent size of the moon is then less than that of the sun and instead of a total eclipse an annular eclipse (*annulus*—a ring) is seen (see Fig. 9).

Eclipse of the moon.

The moon is not self-luminous, but is lit up by the sun. Only that half of the moon facing the sun is illuminated. The phases of the moon are due to the fact that, from the earth, only part of the illuminated half of the moon can, as a rule, be seen. When the moon is on the opposite side of the earth from the sun, we see the whole of the illuminated face of the moon—a full moon. The sun's light is streaming past the earth (but cannot be seen since there are no dust particles to scatter it) and falls upon the moon. If, however, the sun, earth and moon are in a direct line, the light from the sun cannot reach the moon, and the moon is eclipsed.

The umbra in this case is quite large enough for the whole moon to fall well within it. Draw a diagram to represent this. If the moon lies in the penumbra, there is no true eclipse since the whole moon is receiving light from part of the sun. The moon merely becomes less bright. If the moon lies partly in the umbra

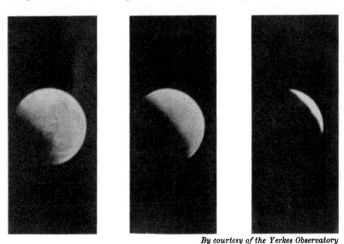

By courtesy of the Yerkes Observatory

Fig. 10. Three phases of an eclipse of the moon. Note the curved shadow of the earth: this affords direct evidence of the sphericity of the earth.

and partly in the penumbra, it is partially eclipsed. The earth's shadow appears to take from it a circular bite, similar to the appearance of the sun when partially eclipsed (see Fig. 10).

Explanation of rectilinear propagation.

The fact that light travels in straight lines is accounted for on the corpuscular theory by assuming that the corpuscles are shot out from a source in straight lines. But there is no simple and straightforward explanation on the wave theory. Indeed, both sound and water waves spread round corners. Newton was unable to detect any evidence of light doing this and in consequence rejected the wave theory, as a complete explanation of light phenomena, in favour of the corpuscular theory.

We have already mentioned, in connection with the pinhole camera, that since Newton's time slight bending of light, called diffraction, has been discovered. The reason why the bending is so small, compared with sound for instance, is because the wavelength of light waves is so minute, a few hundred thousandths of a centimetre. And bending only takes place to a marked extent when light passes through a small aperture or is obstructed by a small obstacle.

A full explanation, on the wave theory, of rectilinear propagation was worked out mathematically by Fresnel, a Frenchman. We can here give only an analogy to illustrate his explanation.

Suppose a number of men in a straight line are advancing abreast. The straight line represents a wave front. The path of each man at right angles to the line represents a ray, and since all the paths are parallel a straight wave front represents a parallel beam of light. Suppose each man, like a wave, has no special tendency to travel in one particular direction. He will nevertheless have to move straight forward because any tendency to move sideways will be obstructed by his neighbours. Similarly light waves do not spread sideways because waves in such directions are destroyed by interference.

Now suppose the line of men encounter a wall in which there is a gateway through which only two men can pass. Once these two men are through they will be able to spread out since they have no neighbours to keep them going straight. This illustrates diffraction (see Plate I (b), facing p. 32).

The velocity of light.

At one time it seemed as if the passage of light was instantaneous.

Galileo made an attempt to measure its velocity but it travelled far too quickly for him. Two observers with lanterns were stationed at night on distant hill-tops. The first observer unshuttered his lantern and simultaneously noted the time. The second observer on seeing the light unshuttered his lantern and the first observer noted the time when he saw the return flash. No consistent results were obtained, and it was realised that the experimenters were merely measuring how quickly the second observer could manipulate his lantern and the first observer read the time.

The principle of this method has since been employed successfully, using a mirror to reflect back the light in place of the second observer and a toothed wheel or mirror rotating at very high speed to measure the time (since the most delicate stopwatches are completely useless).

Astronomical methods.

The first determination of the velocity of light was made in 1675 by the Danish astronomer Roemer, who estimated the time light takes to travel the diameter of the earth's orbit, about 200 million miles, from observations of the eclipses of one of the satellites of Jupiter.

His value was only approximately accurate, but it was of the right order. The correct value is 186,000 miles per sec., or 300,000,000 metres per sec.

Although light was known to travel at an enormous speed, this staggering figure was too much for many of Roemer's contemporaries, and it was not until the English astronomer Bradley in 1728 confirmed his value by a different astronomical method that the value was generally accepted.

Bradley observed that the apparent directions of the fixed stars change slightly during a year. The effect is known as *aberration,* and is of the order of 20 seconds of angle.

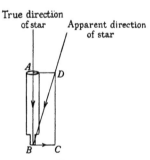

It is said that the explanation of the phenomenon occurred to Bradley while he was boating on the Thames. He noticed that the direction of the wind, as indicated by the flag at the mast-head, seemed to change when the boat began to move, and also each time the boat altered its course. Similarly the apparent direction of the light from the stars changes as the earth moves round its orbit.

Fig. 11

Suppose, in Fig. 11, while the light from a star travels from *A* to *B*, down the telescope, the whole telescope moves bodily from *AB* to *DC* owing to the motion of the earth round the sun. The apparent direction of the light will be *DB* and the telescope must be tilted in this direction for the star to be seen in the middle of the eyepiece—just as an umbrella must be slanted forwards when a person walks briskly in vertically falling rain.

Now light travels a distance *AB* while the earth moves a distance *BC*.

Hence $\qquad \dfrac{\text{Velocity of the earth}}{\text{Velocity of light}} = \dfrac{BC}{AB} = \tan A\hat{B}D.$

Thus, knowing the velocity of the earth (19 miles per sec.) and the angle *ABD* (which is half the angle between the extreme apparent positions of the star when the earth is moving in opposite directions), it is possible to calculate the velocity of light.

Fizeau's terrestrial method.

In 1849 Fizeau devised an accurate method of timing light over a comparatively short distance by means of a rapidly rotating wheel and made the first terrestrial determination of its velocity.

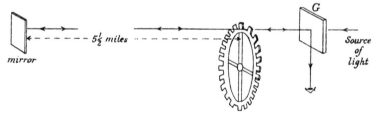

Fig. 12

A narrow beam of light was passed through the glass plate *G* (see Fig. 12) and then through a gap between the teeth of the wheel. After traversing a distance of about $5\frac{1}{2}$ miles and being reflected back by a mirror, it passed through the same gap once more—so long as the wheel had not moved appreciably—and was reflected by the face of the glass plate to the eye, as shown in Fig. 12. The speed of the wheel was then increased until no light reached the eye. This meant that a tooth had taken the place of the gap, through which the light had passed on its out-ward journey, and blocked the return of the light. Knowing the speed of rotation and the number of teeth on the wheel, Fizeau was able to calculate the time taken by the light to cover its double journey.

His wheel had 720 teeth. Hence the distance between the middle of a gap and the middle of an adjacent tooth was $\frac{1}{1440}$th of the circumference. The requisite speed of the wheel was found to be 12·6 rev. per sec.

$$\therefore \text{ Time taken for } 1 \text{ revolution} = \frac{1}{12\cdot6} \text{ sec.}$$

$$\text{,, \quad ,, \quad } \tfrac{1}{1440} \text{ ,, } = \frac{1}{12\cdot6 \times 1440} \text{ sec.}$$

Total distance travelled by the light in this time
$$= 10\cdot7 \text{ miles.}$$

Hence velocity of light
$$= 10\cdot7 \times 12\cdot6 \times 1440$$
$$= 194{,}000 \text{ miles per sec.}$$

A recent determination of the velocity of light was made by Michelson (in 1924–6) using a revolving mirror to time light over a distance of 22 miles and back. This was a modification of a method first used by Foucault.

Summary

Light is a form of energy. According to the *corpuscular theory* it consists of corpuscles or photons and according to the *wave theory* of waves in an all-pervading medium called the aether. The photo-electric effect can be explained satisfactorily only on the former, and interference on the latter, theory.

Light travels in straight lines. This is proved by the formation of sharp shadows and the action of the pinhole camera. Eclipses are caused by shadows cast by the moon, earth, etc. When an extended source is used a shadow consists of umbra and penumbra.

The velocity of light is 186,000 miles per sec., or 300,000,000 metres per sec. It has been determined by Bradley and Fizeau using astronomical and terrestrial methods, respectively.

QUESTIONS

1. Show, with the aid of diagrams, why with a source larger than the obstacle, the shadow is practically all umbra when the obstacle is near the screen, but all penumbra when far away from it.

2. (a) Draw rays showing the umbra and penumbra when the source is larger than the object.

(b) Explain, with diagrams, what the eye sees as it moves from the outside edge of the penumbra to the centre of the umbra. What does it see if it is beyond the apex of the umbra?

(c) What would be the effect on the shadow of gradually covering the source by lowering a blind?

3. A small pinhole is made in the blind of a darkened room on a summer day, when the sun is shining brightly, but is not in front of the window. The room has no furniture and its walls are smooth and white. Describe what would be seen by a person in the room. Could a similar effect be produced by a lens? If so, what kind of lens would be required?   (O.)

4. Explain carefully, with the aid of diagrams, what happens to the image in a pinhole camera:
   (a) when the camera is made longer;
   (b) when the pinhole is square instead of round;
   (c) when the pinhole is gradually increased in size;
   (d) when there are two pinholes close together.

5. In a pinhole camera the distance between the pinhole and the plate is 2 in. and the plate is $3\frac{1}{2}$ in. long. In order to take a full-length portrait of a man 6 ft. tall what is the shortest possible distance between the man and the camera?

6. Describe a method by means of which the velocity of light has been determined.

7. How long does light take to reach the earth:
   (a) from the moon which is 250,000 miles away;
   (b) from the sun which is 93,000,000 miles away?

8. A sharp sound made in a cave is often followed by reverberation owing to successive reflection at opposite walls. At each reflection a certain percentage of the sound energy is absorbed until eventually the sound is too weak to be heard. Why is no similar effect observed when a lamp, situated between parallel mirrors, is switched off?

Chapter II

REFLECTION

Since a non-luminous body such as a sheet of paper is visible from all directions when a beam of light shines upon it, light must proceed in all directions from the surface of the paper. The phenomenon, to which we referred in Chapter I, is known as scattering, or diffuse reflection.

Sometimes the paper seems to "shine" in a particular direction. The effect may be observed with a blackboard. This is due to the fact that light is being reflected more copiously in that direction than in any other. A highly polished body, such as a plane mirror, on which a beam of light is shining, reflects practically all the light at a particular angle: when it is viewed from this angle, the eye is dazzled. The phenomenon is called *regular reflection.*

Experimental investigation of reflection.

A narrow beam of light, obtained by means of a lamp and vertical slit (see Fig. 13), may be reflected at a plane mirror and the directions of the beam before and after reflection marked on a sheet of paper.

The ray falling upon the mirror is termed the *incident ray* and the angle between the perpendicular to the mirror, called the *normal,* and the incident ray is called the *angle of incidence.* Fig. 14 shows also the *reflected ray* and the *angle of reflection.*

Laws of reflection.

When a regular reflection takes place, two laws, called the Laws of Reflection, are always obeyed.

1. The incident ray, the normal, and the reflected ray are in the same plane.

Thus a ray incident on the mirror in the plane of the paper is never reflected up out of the paper.

2. The angle of reflection is equal to the angle of incidence.

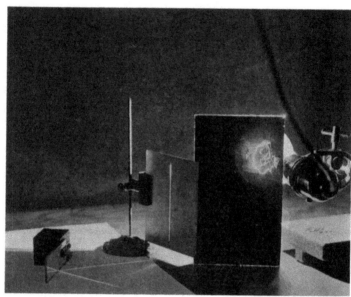

D. G. A. Dyson

Fig. 13. A lamp (shielded from the camera by a piece of red glass) and a vertical slit projecting a beam of light on to a sheet of white paper. The beam is here allowed to fall upon a plane mirror, to illustrate the laws of reflection.

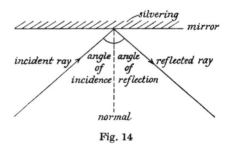

Fig. 14

Image in a plane mirror.

When you look into a plane mirror you see an image of yourself. Where exactly is this image, and how is it formed?

Let us take the simplest possible case, a point object, *O*, the image of which, in a plane mirror, is viewed by an eye *BD* (see Fig. 15). *O* is sending out rays in all directions, but only those lying between *OAB* and *OCD* enter the eye after being reflected at the mirror.

Now the reflected rays *AB* and *CD* both appear to the eye to be coming from *I*, their point of intersection. It can be shown to follow as a geometrical consequence of the laws of reflection that

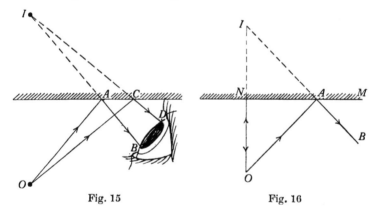

Fig. 15   Fig. 16

all rays from O after reflection at the mirror appear to be coming from I, i.e. if produced backwards they would all intersect in *I*. *I* is called the *image* of *O* in the mirror. It must be observed that the rays produced behind a mirror are always dotted. They do not actually penetrate behind the mirror and are called *virtual* rays. Similarly the image *I* is called a *virtual image*, because it has no objective existence, i.e. it exists only in the mind. It cannot be thrown on to a screen. If you go behind the mirror to the spot where the image appears to be it is impossible to detect any trace of it.

We will now show, by a geometrical proof that **I (the virtual image) is as far behind the mirror as O is in front.**

A ray *ON* (see Fig. 16) which strikes the mirror normally will be reflected back along its own path. Another ray OA is reflected along AB. I is the point of intersection of ON and BA produced.

We require to prove that $IN = ON$.

Proof. By the laws of reflection

$$N\hat{A}O = M\hat{A}B = \text{vertically opposite } I\hat{A}N.$$

In the $\triangle$s IAN, OAN, NA is common.

$$I\hat{N}A = O\hat{N}A = 90°,$$
$$I\hat{A}N = N\hat{A}O.$$
$$\therefore \; \triangle \, IAN \equiv \triangle \, OAN.$$
$$\therefore \; IN = ON.$$

Since OA may be any ray from O, this proof holds for all rays from O. Thus we may deduce that all reflected rays, if produced back, would pass through one point, I.

Image of a line.

In Fig. 17 $A'B'$ is the image in a plane mirror of the line AB. Rays are drawn showing how an eye sees the image. Two rays

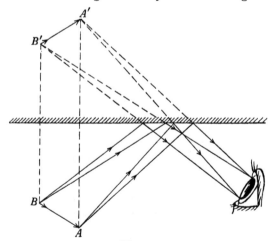

Fig. 17

are drawn from both A and B, and after reflection in the mirror appear to be coming from their points of intersection, A' and B'.

The figure is most easily drawn *not* by making the angles of reflection of the rays equal to the angles of incidence, but by fixing first the position of the image $A'B'$, knowing that A' and B' are as far behind the mirror as A and B are in front. Then the direction of the reflected rays may be obtained from the position of the image.

Lateral inversion.

If a page of print is held in front of a mirror the image of the print seen in the mirror is reversed. One of the more elementary tricks in the detective's repertoire is to read the culprit's correspondence by holding up the blotter to a mirror.

This sideways reversal of the image is known as *lateral inversion*. How are we to explain it? Suppose a man with a monocle in his right eye looks into a mirror. The monocle appears to be in the left eye of the image. Since his face is nearer the mirror than the back of his head, and each part of the image is formed as far behind the mirror as that part of the object is in front, the person appears to be facing in the opposite direction. Thus the eye which is directly opposite the right eye of the object is the left eye of the image. All lateral inversion is in fact due to the image facing out of the mirror while the object faces into it. A rubber stamp has to be laterally inverted for the same reason.

Two parallel mirrors.

On looking into a mirror which is faced by a parallel mirror on the opposite wall you can see a very large number of images of the room stretching away in an apparently endless vista. If the mirrors are accurately parallel you can see only one image of yourself (since this covers all the rest) but a companion standing beside you would tell you that a whole series of alternate front and back views of your person were visible to him. How are these formed?

To simplify the problem we will take a point object O (see Fig. 18). O gives rise to an image I_1 in the mirror M_1 as far behind the mirror as O is in front. But the image I_1 gives rise to another image I_{12} in M_2, I_{12} gives rise to an image I_{121} in M_1 and so on. There is therefore a series of images in both mirrors representing that side of O facing the mirror M_1 which we may call the "front view" of O. There is also another series of images, I_2, I_{21}, I_{212}, starting with the image of the "back view" of O in M_2, I_2. These images are all "back views" of O. The light by means of which an eye sees these images must have originated at O. It is reflected backwards and forwards between the mirrors. See Plate II(*d*), facing p. 33.

In Fig. 18 the rays are drawn by which an eye sees I_{12}. As the notation suggests, rays from O are reflected first at M_1 (after which they appear to come from the first image I_1) and then at M_2: on entering the eye, they appear to be diverging from I_{12}. It

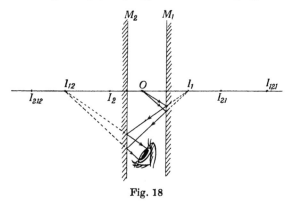

Fig. 18

should be remembered that O is giving out rays in all directions, but only those which after these reflections enter the eye are drawn. If the eye were moved it would see I_{12} by means of an entirely different set of rays.

Two inclined mirrors.

On looking into two mirrors inclined at 60° you see five images of yourself. Fig. 19(*a*) shows how these are formed. The positions of the images may be determined most easily by drawing a circle, taking two radii inclined at 60° as the positions of the mirrors, and taking a point O on the circumference as the object. Since a chord perpendicular to a radius is bisected by it, and the line joining an object and its image formed in a plane mirror is perpendicularly bisected by the mirror, all the images must lie on the circumference of the circle.

In Fig. 19(a), O gives rise to an image I_1 in the mirror M_1, I_1 to I_{12} in M_2, and I_{12} to I_{121} in M_1. It will be seen that although I_{12} is beyond the end of M_1 it is nevertheless in front of it, and consequently gives rise to an image. On the other hand, I_{121} is behind both mirrors and cannot give rise to further images.

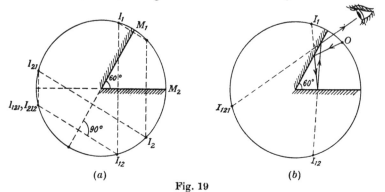

Fig. 19

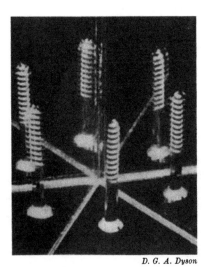

D. G. A. Dyson

Fig. 20. The five images of a screw in two plane mirrors inclined at 60°. (See Fig. 19.)

Similarly O gives rise to I_2 in M_2, I_2 to I_{21} in M_1, and I_{21} to I_{212} in M_2. When the mirrors are inclined accurately at 60° the images I_{121} and I_{212} coincide.

The number of images formed by two mirrors inclined at an angle of $\theta°$ is given by the formula

$$n = \frac{360}{\theta} - 1.$$

Thus when $\theta = 60°$, $n = \frac{360}{60} - 1 = 5$.

As in the case of parallel mirrors the rays by which an eye sees the various images are reflected successively at the two mirrors. Fig. 19 (b) shows a ray by means of which the eye sees the image I_{121}, and Plate II (c), facing p. 33, is a photograph of an actual beam incident in a similar position. Fig. 20 shows the five images of a screw in two mirrors at 60^c.

Pepper's ghost.

A plane transparent sheet of glass will act as a mirror. Thus on dark winter afternoons the fire in a room may, on looking through the window, be seen burning in the street, the window acting as a mirror.

The idea has been utilised by the illusionist Prof. Pepper, to create a ghost. A large vertical sheet of glass is placed at 45° to the front of a stage. A man, M, suitably dressed and illuminated, stands in the wings and the audience see his image in the glass G, the ghost (see Fig. 21). Other actors can walk behind the glass and pass apparently right through the ghost, which is also semi-transparent. The footlights are not lighted, and the audience is unaware of the presence of the glass.

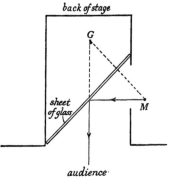

Fig. 21. Pepper's ghost.

A rotating mirror.

Using the apparatus shown in Fig. 13, allow a "ray" to fall on a plane mirror and mark the position of the reflected ray.

Turn the mirror through a measured angle α (keeping the direction of the incident ray fixed), and determine the angle turned through by the reflected ray. You may be surprised to find that it is 2α. This fact may be deduced assuming the laws of reflection:

Suppose a ray PO falls perpendicularly on a plane mirror AOB. It is reflected back along its own path. The mirror is now turned through an angle α, so that its new position is $A'OB'$. If ON is the normal to

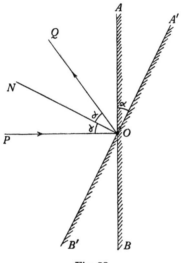

Fig. 22

the mirror in its new position, then PON is equal to α since the normal must have turned through the same angle as the mirror.

OQ is the new position of the reflected ray.

By the second law of reflection

$$Q\hat{O}N = P\hat{O}N.$$

∴ Angle through which the reflected ray is turned, POQ, is equal to 2α.

We have here considered the special case of ray originally normal to the mirror. The student who is proficient in geometry should try to prove the proposition taking an incident ray originally inclined to the normal.

The small deflection of the coil of a sensitive galvanometer (for measuring minute electric currents) is often obtained by reflecting a beam of light from a mirror attached to the coil. Allowance has to be made for the fact that the reflected beam, acting as a pointer, turns through an angle twice that turned through by the coil.

The sextant.

The sextant is an instrument employed in navigation for finding the altitude of the sun and stars and also in surveying. It uses the principle just proved, that the angle turned through by a plane mirror is equal to half the angle turned through by the reflected ray.

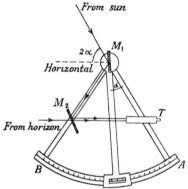

Fig. 23. The sextant.

It is represented in Fig. 23. A plane mirror M_1 is fixed to an arm which can be rotated, and the angle of rotation measured on a circular scale. The mirror M_2, which has one half silvered and the other half transparent, is fixed to the framework and cannot rotate. The telescope T is also fixed.

When the end of the rotating arm is pushed up against A the mirrors M_1 and M_2 are parallel. Light, therefore, after successive reflection at M_1 and M_2 enters the telescope parallel to its original direction. Thus, on looking through the telescope, two coincident images of the horizon may be seen, one formed by light reflected at M_1 and M_2 and the other by light passing through the unsilvered portion of M_2.

In order to find the elevation of the sun the moving arm is rotated until the image of the sun, formed by light reflected at M_1 and M_2, coincides in position with the image of the horizon formed by light passing through the unsilvered part of M_2. Then

Fig. 24. A ship's officer finding the altitude of the sun by means of a sextant.

the angle turned through by the rotating arm is equal to half the angle of elevation required (marked 2α in Fig. 23), since the angle turned through by the mirror is equal to half the angle between the two incident rays, the reflected ray being fixed. For this reason, each degree on the circular scale of the sextant is marked as two degrees.

Fig. 24 shows a ship's officer taking readings of the sun's elevation with a sextant. From these readings, taken at noon, the latitude of a place may be determined. The light from the sun is viewed through coloured glass to reduce its intensity. The great advantage of the sextant is that accurate measurements can be taken with it even while it is in constant movement due to the motion of the ship.

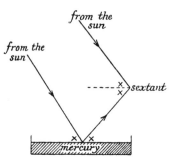

Fig. 25

At sea, the horizon is where sky and water meet, but on land an artificial horizon must be used. Advantage is taken of the fact that the surface of a still liquid is accurately horizontal. The mirror M_1 of the sextant is moved so that the sun appears to coincide in position, not with the horizon, but with the image of itself so formed, using the surface of mercury as a mirror. It is clear from Fig. 25 that the angle between the two rays entering the sextant is equal to twice the elevation of the sun.

Explanation of reflection.

To explain reflection on the corpuscular theory, the corpuscles are assumed to be perfectly elastic. They bounce on a plane mirror rather as a billiard ball rebounds from the cushion of a billiard table. The billiard ball obeys the laws of reflection approximately and would obey them exactly if it were perfectly elastic.

The wave theory also provides a complete and satisfactory explanation of reflection. We shall content ourselves here with demonstrating experimentally that waves obey the laws of reflection.

The reflection of waves at a plane surface may be shown by means of the ripple tank (see p. 3). Plate I(c), facing p. 32, shows the reflection of a straight wave front—corresponding to a parallel beam of light since the rays are everywhere at right angles to the wave front. Note that the inclination to the surface of the reflected waves is equal to that of the incident waves.

SUMMARY

Laws of reflection.

1. The incident ray, the normal, and the reflected ray are in the same plane.

2. The angle of reflection is equal to the angle of incidence.

The image in a plane mirror is as far behind the mirror as the object is in front. It is laterally inverted.

A number of images are formed by two inclined plane mirrors of an object placed between them.

When a mirror is rotated, the position of the incident ray being fixed, the reflected ray turns through twice the angle turned through by the mirror. The sextant is an instrument using this principle.

QUESTIONS

1. State the laws of reflection of light. How can it be proved (*a*) theoretically, and (*b*) experimentally, that the image of a pin in a plane mirror is as far behind the mirror as the object is in front?

(L.)

2. Find the velocity of the image in a plane mirror, with respect to the ground:

(*a*) when a man walks towards the mirror at 6 ft. per sec.;

(*b*) when the mirror is moved towards the man (who stands still) at 6 ft. per sec.

3. Show, with the aid of a diagram, that a man can just see all of himself in a vertical mirror half his height. (To simplify the problem, assume the man's eyes to be at the top of his head. When you have decided where the mirror should be placed and drawn the diagram for this case, try to answer the question assuming the eyes to be in the correct position.)

4. Explain carefully:

(*a*) A long mirror may easily be mistaken for an open door.

(*b*) A plane mirror may be set up where a main road makes a sudden right-angled bend to warn motorists of approaching traffic. Draw a diagram, with rays, to illustrate.

(*c*) An optician, whose consulting room is not long enough for testing eyes, can double the effective length of his room by means of a mirror. Draw a detailed diagram.

(*d*) The image of a man, standing by the side, appears in a still lake to be upside down.

5. A clock (having marks instead of numbers on its dial) appears to indicate 4.35 when viewed in a mirror. What is the correct time?

6. Explain:

(*a*) The method of arranging large mirrors in a tailor's shop so that you may see your own back by reflection.

(*b*) Light is propagated in straight lines, yet every part of a room having only north windows is illuminated at noonday.

(O. & C.)

7. Explain:

(*a*) A sheet of ground glass becomes almost transparent when wet.

(*b*) The image of a right hand formed by a plane mirror looks like a left hand. (C.)

8. Describe an experiment for finding the positions of the image formed by a plane mirror of a pin placed in front of it. What difference would it make whether you were using a polished metal surface, or a piece of thick glass, silvered at the back? (L.)

9. Explain why, on a moonlight night when the surface of the sea is covered with ripples, a band of light can be seen extending towards the moon. How is this formed?

10. When you look in a mirror your image is inverted sideways. Why is it not inverted lengthways also, i.e. turned upside down?

11. A plane mirror 2 ft. high is fixed on one wall of a room, the lower edge being 4 ft. 6 in. from the ground. If the opposite wall of the room is 14 ft. distant and 10 ft. high, draw a diagram to show from what point a man must look in order to see reflected in the mirror the whole height of the opposite wall from floor to ceiling. (L.)

12. How can two plane mirrors be arranged to form a simple periscope? Draw rays showing how a man in a submerged submarine can see an object above the water.

13. Prove that when a plane mirror is rotated the reflected light rotates at twice the rate.

Two plane mirrors are placed back to back and are opened out gradually to form a wedge, the reflecting surfaces being on the outside. A beam of parallel light falls on the edge of the wedge, and it is found that the two beams reflected from its faces make ultimately an angle of 110° with each other. Find the angle between the mirrors, explaining carefully the principle of the method.   (N.)

14. Describe the sextant. How may it be used to find the latitude of a place?

15. Two plane mirrors are inclined at an angle to each other. A ray of light parallel to one of the mirrors travels, after two reflections, parallel to the other. Find the angle between the mirrors.

(O. & C.)

16. Explain the formation of the series of images of an object placed between two parallel mirrors. Draw a diagram showing the pencil of rays by which an eye sees the third image in one of the mirrors. Why is there a limit to the number of images visible?   (L.)

17. State the laws of reflection of light.

A traveller seated in a compartment of a railway corridor coach at night can, if he looks through the window on the corridor side of the coach, see four images of the light in the carriage, two images being bright, and two rather faint. Assuming that none of these images has involved more than two reflections, explain, with the help of ray diagrams, how each of them is formed. Assuming that the width of the compartment is 6 ft., and that of the corridor 2 ft., and that the light is in the centre of the compartment, calculate the positions of the images.   (C.)

18. When you look at the junction of two plane mirrors, set exactly at right angles, you can see your own image. Explain how this image is formed and how it differs from the image seen in a single plane mirror.   (O. & C.)

19. Two mirrors are inclined at 70°. Draw a diagram, accurately to scale, showing the images formed when a point object is placed between them. If instead of a point, a letter *R* were used as an object, draw the appearance of each image.

20. A ray of light, in passing from one point to another, is reflected at a plane mirror. Show, by a geometrical proof, that in obeying the laws of reflection, it is taking the shortest path.

Chapter III

REFRACTION

A ray of light is bent as it passes from one medium to another—from air to water for example (see Plate II (*a*), facing p. 33). The phenomenon is called *refraction*.

In Fig. 26 a number of terms used in connection with refraction are shown. The ray passing from air to water is called the

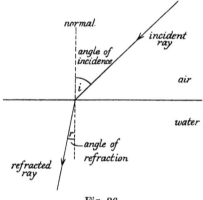

Fig. 26

incident ray. After refraction at the surface it is called the *refracted ray*. The angle between the incident ray and the normal to the surface is called the *angle of incidence*; the angle between the refracted ray and the normal is called the *angle of refraction*.

A ray passing from an optically rarer to an optically denser medium (e.g. from air to water or glass) *is bent towards the normal*, and *vice versa*.

Experimental investigation of refraction.

Using the apparatus shown in Fig. 13 pass a narrow beam of light through a rectangular block of glass.

On emerging (see Fig. 27), the beam will be found to be parallel

PLATE I

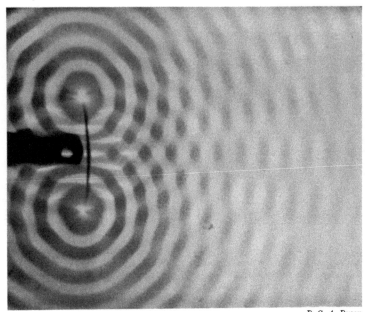

D. G. A. Dyson

(a)

Interference of water waves. (Compare Fig. 3 and see pp. 2–3.)

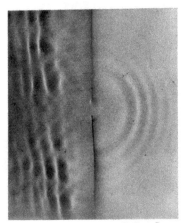

D. G. A. Dyson

(b)

Diffraction of water waves. The straight waves after passing through the small aperture become spherical and spread (see p. 12).

D. G. A. Dyson

(c)

Reflection of water waves (see p. 28). The blacker waves at the top are moving towards the obstacle: the lower waves have been reflected and are moving back. Note that the inclinations of the two sets of waves to the reflector are equal.

PLATE II

D. G. A. Dyson

(a)

The refraction of light on passing from air to water. The water contains eosin which makes it fluoresce in the path of the light.

D. G. A. Dyson

(b)

Total internal reflection. The light strikes the under surface of the water in the tank at an angle of incidence greater than the critical angle.

D. G. A. Dyson

(c)

Reflection of light at two mirrors at 60°. (See p. 23 and compare this with Fig. 19 (b).) Note how the single beam becomes multiple owing to multiple reflections.

D. G. A. Dyson

(d)

Reflection of light at two parallel mirrors. Note the multiple reflected beams and how they lose their intensity at each reflection owing to absorption by the glass.

to its original direction and to have been displaced laterally. Note
the reflected beam where the incident beam strikes the first face
of the block. Reflection and refraction always occur together.
As the face of the block is placed more obliquely to the incident
beam, more light is reflected and less passes through the block.

Mark the positions of the beam and block, and measure the
angles of incidence and refraction (both where the beam enters
and leaves the block). Obtain several different sets of values by
altering the inclination of the block to the incident beam.

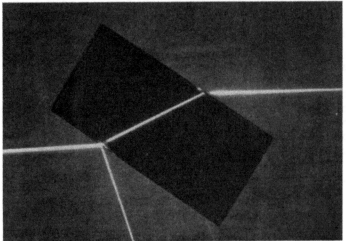

D. G. A. Dyson

Fig. 27. Refraction of light through a parallel-sided slab of glass (the
incident beam is on the left). Note also the reflected beam at the first face
and the faint reflected beam inside the glass at the second face.

The search for a law.

The first recorded observations of angles of incidence and
refraction were made by Ptolemy, a native of Egypt, who taught
in the Greek university of Alexandria during the second century A.D.

Ptolemy tabulated a series of values for light passing from air
to water, air to glass, and water to glass. He searched for a
relation between the angles, but did not find one.

Eight centuries later, during the period of Arab ascendancy, Al Hazen also made a series of determinations of angles of incidence and refraction, but he too failed to find a law connecting them. Kepler, the mathematician and astronomer, spent considerable time testing whether the readings would fit various formulae, and eventually evolved an elaborate expression which held approximately. The exact relation, however, was discovered by Willebrord Snell (1591–1626), a professor of mechanics at Leyden University, some fifteen hundred years after Ptolemy's readings were taken.

The laws of refraction.

1st law. The incident and refracted rays are on opposite sides of and in the same plane as the normal.

2nd law (or Snell's law). When a ray of light passes from one medium to another the sine of the angle of incidence bears a constant ratio to the sine of the angle of refraction. The ratio is called the refractive index from one medium to the other, and is denoted by the Greek letter μ.

Thus
$$\mu = \frac{\sin i}{\sin r}.$$

The value of μ varies for different pairs of media. Thus from air to water $\mu = \frac{4}{3}$ and from air to ordinary crown glass $\mu = \frac{3}{2}$ (approximately).

The readings given in the table below were obtained in an experiment with a block of glass, similar to that described above. The value of $\mu = \dfrac{\sin i}{\sin r}$ has been worked out for each pair of readings of i and r. It will be seen that μ is approximately constant:

i	r	$\sin i$	$\sin r$	$\dfrac{\sin i}{\sin r}$
14°	9°	0·242	0·156	1·56
35°	21½°	0·574	0·366	1·56
49°	29°	0·755	0·485	1·56
59°	33°	0·857	0·545	1·56
69½°	37½°	0·937	0·609	1·54
88°	39½°	0·999	0·636	1·54

Explanation of refraction.

Light bends as it passes, say, from air to water because its velocity in water is less than its velocity in air.

Fig. 28 shows plane light waves passing from air to water. The dotted lines represent the directions of travel of the waves, i.e. rays.

Consider the wave front *AB*, the end *A* of which is just entering the water. While the end *B* travels to *D* in air, the end *A* travels a shorter distance *AC* in water. Consequently the wave is slewed round into the position *CD*, the positions intermediate between *AB* and *CD* being shown in the figure.

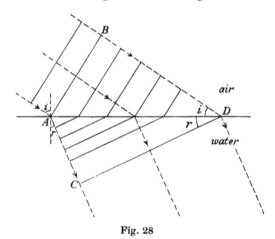

Fig. 28

If μ is the refractive index from air to water, it can be proved that

$$\mu = \frac{\text{Velocity of light in air}}{\text{Velocity of light in water}}.$$

The student should verify this for himself by proving that, in Fig. 28,

$$\frac{\sin i}{\sin r} = \frac{BD}{AC}.$$

The refraction of water waves may be demonstrated by placing in the ripple tank a plane slab of glass causing the water above it to become shallow. Since the velocity of waves in shallow water is less than in deeper water, refraction takes place when waves reach the edge of the glass (see Fig. 29 and Plate IV, facing p. 65).

Newton explained refraction on the corpuscular theory by assuming that the velocity of light in a denser medium, such as

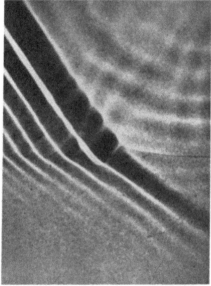

D. G. A. Dyson

Fig. 29. The refraction of straight water waves. The waves are moving down from the N.E. corner of this photograph: on entering shallower water they travel more slowly and are slewed round (or refracted) in consequence.

water, is greater than that in air. When, in 1850, Foucault found experimentally that this was not the case, it was regarded as a decisive blow to the corpuscular theory. But it was a knock-out long after defeat on points, for the corpuscular theory had been abandoned fifty years earlier, owing to its inability to account for interference.

Multiple images.

Place a candle flame near to a thick glass mirror. Look in the mirror obliquely. Several images of the candle flame will be seen, the second from the front being the brightest (see Fig. 30).

The way in which these images are formed is shown in Fig. 31. The first image I_1 is formed by reflection at the front surface of the glass. The second image I_2 is formed by the light which enters the glass and is reflected once at the silvering. I_3 is formed by light which is reflected at the silvering, then at the inside surface of the front of the glass and once more at the silvering.

B. F. Brown

Fig. 30.   Multiple images of a candle flame in a thick glass mirror.
(See Fig. 31).

Reflection continues inside the glass and further images are seen until the light becomes too dim. This recalls the effect described on p. 21. Which is the image we normally see?

Apparent depth.

Owing to refraction, a stream does not appear to be as deep as it really is. The rays by means of which an object under water, O, is viewed (see Fig. 32) do not travel straight to the eye, but are bent as they leave the surface. When produced back they intersect in I. O appears to be at I, the point from which both rays seem to come, therefore, and I is called the image of O by refraction.

When we were considering the image of a point object formed by reflection in a plane mirror, we were able to prove geometrically, assuming the laws of reflection to be true, that all rays from the object, after reflection at the mirror, when produced back, must intersect in one point, the image; that is to say they all appear to come from a single point whose position is the same from wherever we look at it. In the case of an image formed by

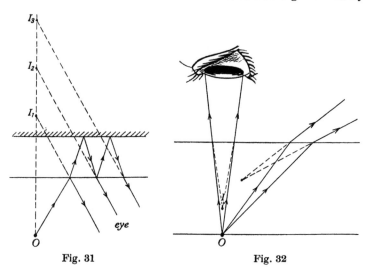

Fig. 31   Fig. 32

refraction, however, all the refracted rays do not pass through one point. In Fig. 32 a second pair of rays are drawn by means of which an eye would view O from an oblique position. The image appears to be at the point of intersection of the refracted rays and this point does not coincide with I. In fact the position of the image changes as the position of the eye changes. A stream appears even less deep when viewed obliquely than when viewed vertically from above. As the eye moves the image traces out a curve called a caustic, I being known as the cusp (see Fig. 33).

There is a simple relation between the real depth and apparent

depth when the eye looks vertically down into a transparent
medium, such as water or glass, of refractive index μ:

$$\frac{\text{Real depth}}{\text{Apparent depth}} = \mu.$$

Thus, since $\mu = \frac{4}{3}$, the apparent depth of a stream viewed
vertically is $\frac{3}{4}$ of the real depth.

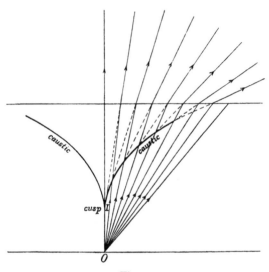

Fig. 33

In Fig. 34 OA is a ray from an object O on the bed of a stream,
which strikes the surface of the water at right angles and passes through
undeviated. Another ray slightly inclined to the first, OB, is refracted along BC, and when produced back intersects OA in I. I is
therefore the image of O.

In this figure we require to prove that $\dfrac{AO}{AI} = \mu$.

Now $A\hat{O}B = O\hat{B}N = r$ (alternate angles).
Similarly

$A\hat{I}B = $ alternate $I\hat{B}N = $ vert. opp. $M\hat{B}C = i$.

In rt. angled $\triangle$ *ABI*, $\sin i = \dfrac{AB}{BI}$.

,,   ,, $\triangle$ *ABO*, $\sin r = \dfrac{AB}{BO}$.

$\therefore \ \mu = \dfrac{\sin i}{\sin r} = \dfrac{\dfrac{AB}{BI}}{\dfrac{AB}{BO}} = \dfrac{BO}{BI} = \dfrac{AO}{AI}$ approximately, when the eye looks

vertically downwards.

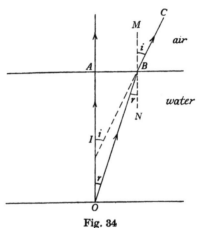

Fig. 34

Total internal reflection.

On passing from water to air, a ray of light perpendicular to the surface travels straight on without being bent. A ray inclined to the normal is bent away from the normal. Thus in Fig. 35 the ray *OP* is refracted into the direction *PQ*. As the inclination to the normal is increased, there is a position in which the refracted ray lies along the surface of the water. Thus the ray *OR* is refracted along *RS*. The angle *ORN* is called the *critical angle, C.* A ray, *OT*, making a greater angle with the normal than *C* cannot get through the surface, and is *totally internally reflected* along *TV*.

Plate II (*b*), facing p. 33, is a photograph of a beam of light being totally internally reflected in water containing a trace of eosin.

Now a ray of light is reversible. Thus in Fig. 35 a ray in the direction SR would be refracted along RO. In this case, $i=90°$, $r=C$.

If $\mu =$ refractive index from air to water,

$$\mu = \frac{\sin i}{\sin r} = \frac{\sin 90°}{\sin C}.$$

But $$\sin 90° = 1.$$

$$\therefore \ \sin C = \frac{1}{\mu}.$$

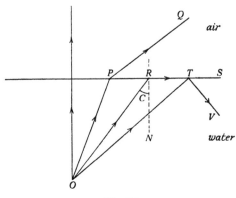

Fig. 35

We can from this simple formula, knowing the refractive index of water to be $\frac{4}{3}$, calculate the critical angle:

$$\sin C = \frac{1}{4/3} = 0.75.$$

$$\therefore \ C = 48° \ 35'.$$

Calculate for yourself the critical angle for glass of refractive index 1·5.

On the other hand a determination of C enables μ to be calculated. This is the basis of most commercial instruments for determining μ, since only a single measurement is required and the instrument can be made to read direct in terms of μ.

Experiment with a test-tube.

Hold an empty test-tube partially immersed and inclined to the surface of water in a glass beaker. Allow light from a lantern or a window to fall in a horizontal direction on the side of the beaker (see Fig. 36). On looking vertically down, the test-tube appears to be brightly silvered owing to the fact that light cannot be refracted into the air inside the test-tube, and is totally internally reflected. If the test-tube is filled with water very little reflection takes place and the bright silvery surface disappears.

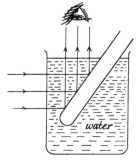

Fig. 36

The metallic appearance of a crack in plate glass is due to the same cause.

Totally reflecting prisms.

The critical angle for crown glass is about 42°. Hence light incident normally on one face of a 90°–45° glass prism makes an angle with the normal at the further face greater than the critical angle. It is therefore totally internally reflected (see Fig. 37). Such prisms act as efficient mirrors, and are often used in that capacity in optical instruments. They have no silvering to tarnish and give rise to a single instead of multiple reflections.

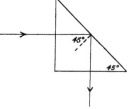

Fig. 37

An inverted image (for instance that produced by an optical lantern) may be made erect by means of a prism (see Fig. 38(a) and (b)). Erecting prisms are used in prismatic binoculars, as we shall see in Chapter X.

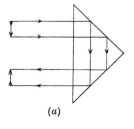

(a)

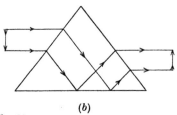

(b)

Fig. 38

The fish's-eye view.

As a result of refraction and total internal reflection, the fish has a very distorted view of things beyond the confines of its watery world.

Light from the horizon falling on the surface of the water is refracted at an angle of 48° 35′ to the normal (the critical angle for water). The setting sun, therefore, to the fish, appears to be

B. F. Brown

Fig. 39. A fish's view of a ring of boys when it looks upwards. The photograph was taken with a pinhole camera filled with water, as described in Prof. R. W. Wood's book, *Physical Optics*. The camera was raised about 9 inches from the ground since if it were placed on the ground the photograph depicts monstrous legs and very small heads.

at this elevation, and so does the whole circle of the horizon. The fish on looking up at the surface of the water sees a bright circular hole, as it were, subtending a semi-vertical angle of 48° 35′ at its eye. Beyond this bright circle no light can penetrate, and all is comparatively dark, except for faint images seen by reflection of

44   LIGHT

objects on the bottom. In the bright circle the whole of the outside world is compressed (see Figs. 39 and 40).

The luminous jet.

Fig. 41 is a picture of what is called the luminous jet. A horizontal beam of light is projected into a jet of water issuing from a horizontal spout. If the water is flowing at a certain speed, where

B. F. Brown

Fig. 40. A fish's view of a straight row of boys when it looks out of the side of an aquarium. A pinhole camera, filled with water, was placed, waist high. a few feet in front of the boys. (See also Fig. 39.)

the jet bends over the light is totally internally reflected, since it makes an angle greater than the critical angle, with the normal to the surface. The light then suffers successive total internal reflections, and is trapped in the jet until the latter strikes the ground, upon which a pool of light is shed. If the jet quivers or breaks up, it sparkles as light darts momentarily out of the surface. The effect is sometimes seen when water is poured out of a jug.

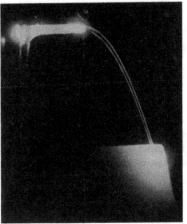

B. F. Brown

Fig. 41. The luminous jet. Light from a lantern shines into the horizontal glass tube at the top. This light is trapped in the water jet, owing to total internal reflection, and makes a pool of light where the jet strikes a white tile.

Fig. 42 shows a bent glass rod devised by Messrs C. Baker for use as a microscope slide illuminator. Light from the lamp is trapped in the rod as in the luminous jet and is reflected up through the microscope slide.

Fig. 42

A very similar piece of glass, attached to a small pocket lamp, is also used by some doctors for illuminating the back of a patient's throat.

Precious stones.

The brilliancy of the diamond is due to its high refractive index (2·42) and therefore small critical angle. The stone is cut

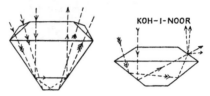

Fig. 43

so that light which has entered it is totally internally reflected many times and is emitted only in certain directions (see Fig. 43). The emitted beams are very intense and cause the gem to sparkle.

Atmospheric refraction.

1. *Apparent elevation of a star.* Air is less dense at a great height than at sea level. At the summit of Mount Everest, for instance, its density is only one-quarter of its density at sea level.

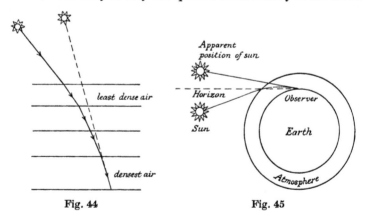

Fig. 44　　　　　　　　　　　　　　Fig. 45

Thus light coming from a star progresses continuously from rarer to slightly denser media. Let us imagine, for simplicity, that the atmosphere is made up of horizontal layers of uniform density (see Fig. 44). A ray of light from a star is gradually bent towards the normal with the result that the star appears higher in the sky than it really is. The bending is greatest when the star is near the horizon—about 36', an angle greater than that subtended by the sun. This has to be allowed for by ships' officers in determining the altitude of the sun or a star and also of course by astronomers.

2. *The setting sun.* As a result of atmospheric refraction the sun is visible above the horizon for some time after it has theoretically set in the evening, and also before it has theoretically risen in the morning. Fig. 45 shows how the rays from the sun are bent in the earth's atmosphere. If the atmosphere could be removed the sun would be invisible. The phenomenon results in a lengthening of the day by 7 or 8 minutes.

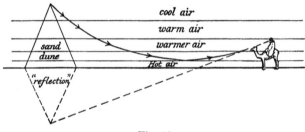

Fig. 46

3. *The mirage.* The best known example of atmospheric refraction is the mirage in the desert. The traveller sees in the distance what seems to be a shimmering lake in which the surrounding sand-dunes are reflected. But the lake is an image of the sky by refraction and the "reflections" have a similar origin.

Fig. 46 shows what is happening. The desert sand becomes very hot, and causes the air near the ground to become hotter and therefore less dense than the air above it. In Fig. 46, for simplicity, the air is represented in layers although actually there is a gradual change in temperature. Now light from the sky or the top of a dune entering the cool air in a particular direction will become bent "away from the normal" until on reaching the lowest layer of hot air it is making an angle with the normal greater than the critical angle. It is there totally internally reflected, and as it passes into the cooler air again it is bent "towards the normal". To the observer in Fig. 46 the top of the dune appears to lie along the final direction of the light as it enters his eye. The dune therefore appears upside down. The light from the sky behind the dune appears to be coming also from the ground and gives the impression of a lake. Only rays in a certain direction are totally internally reflected so that only part of the sky forms an image and the lake is of limited extent. By direct rays the observer can see the dune upright, and the sky behind it. See the picture between pp. 48 and 49.

A tiny mirage can sometimes be seen on a tar-macadam road in summer particularly when the vision is very oblique—as in ascending a hill. Small puddles appear in the distance, which on a closer inspection are found to be non-existent.

A mirage sometimes occurs over the sea, when images of ships are seen in the sky. In this case the air near the sea is colder than that above it and light is refracted and totally internally reflected in a manner similar to that just described. Draw a diagram to illustrate this phenomenon.

Refraction through a prism.

Using the apparatus shown in Fig. 13, pass a narrow beam of light through a glass prism, placing the prism in a position similar to Fig. 47. The light on entering the prism is bent towards the normal and on leaving the prism it is bent away from the normal. The angle between the incident and emergent rays is called the *angle of deviation.*

If the prism is turned slowly, the direction of the incident ray remaining fixed, the direction of the emergent ray changes. Suppose the prism is turned in such a direction that the emergent ray is, as it were, slowly moving "up" so that the angle of deviation is decreased. There comes a time when, in whatever direction the prism is turned, the emergent ray will not move any further in this direction but begins to return. *The deviation is then a minimum.* It can be shown both experimentally and mathematically that in the position of minimum deviation the emergent and incident rays are equally inclined to the surface of the prism, and if the prism is isosceles, the ray inside the glass is parallel to the base of the prism.

There is a relation between the angle of minimum deviation D,

Photograph of a mirage, taken in the Persian desert. There appears to be a la

By courtesy of Prof. A. O. Rankine

near the horizon, in which may be seen "reflections" of the hills (see p. 48).

the refracting angle A of the prism (marked in Fig. 48), and the refractive index of the glass μ:

$$\mu = \frac{\sin \dfrac{A+D}{2}}{\sin \dfrac{A}{2}}.$$

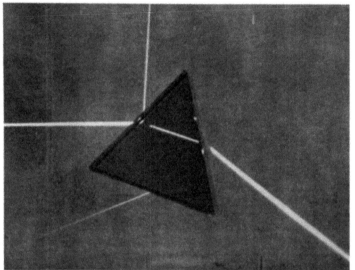

Fig. 47. Refraction of light through a glass prism; (the incident beam is on the left). Note also the reflection (1) at the first face of the prism, (2) at the second inside face giving rise to an emergent beam through the base.

In Fig. 48 $PQRS$ is a ray passing through the prism in the minimum deviation (i.e. symmetrical) position. QO and RO are normals at Q and R respectively.

Hence $\qquad\qquad P\hat{Q}N = S\hat{R}M = i.$

Also $\qquad\qquad O\hat{Q}R = O\hat{R}Q = r.$

$\qquad \therefore\ L\hat{Q}R = L\hat{R}Q = i - r.$

Since in the quadrilateral $AQOR$

$$A\hat{Q}O = A\hat{R}O = 90°,$$
$$Q\hat{O}R = 180° - A.$$

Since the sum of the angles of $\triangle QRO$ is $180°$

$$180 - A + 2r = 180°.$$

$$\therefore \quad r = \frac{A}{2}.$$

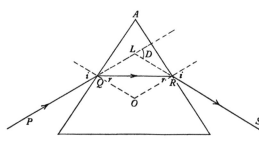

Fig. 48

Again, in the $\triangle LQR$,

$$D = 2(i - r) \quad \text{[exterior angle = sum of interior}$$
$$\text{opposite angles].}$$

$$\therefore \quad 2i = D + 2r = D + A.$$

$$\therefore \quad i = \frac{A + D}{2}.$$

$$\therefore \quad \mu = \frac{\sin i}{\sin r} = \frac{\sin \dfrac{A + D}{2}}{\sin \dfrac{A}{2}}.$$

It is thus possible to calculate the refractive index of the glass of a prism if A and D are found experimentally. D may be found by measuring the angle between the incident and emergent light beams when the prism is turned into the minimum deviation position as described at the beginning of this section.

The angle A may be found by reflecting two parallel beams of light from the two faces bounding it (see Fig. 49). The angle between the two reflected rays (those outside the prism) is equal to $2A$. See if you can prove this assuming the laws of reflection.

The most accurate way of finding A and D by the above methods is to use a spectrometer (see p. 121).

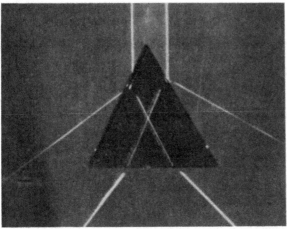

D. G. A. Dyson

Fig. 49. Determination of the angle of a prism by reflecting two parallel beams at the faces bounding it. (Ignore the refracted rays inside the prism and the emergent beams through the base.) The angle of the prism is half the angle between the reflected rays.

Lighting basements by prismatic glass.

Ribbed glass, acting like a large number of prisms, is sometimes used for diffusing light into a basement. Fig. 50 shows how light which is almost vertical is deviated sideways into a room.

Industrial importance of refractive index.

Makers of lenses and optical instruments require to determine accurately the refractive index of all the glass they use. The method they adopt is the prism method described above.

The purity and concentration of such diverse substances as milk, butter, margarine, vegetable oils, sugar solutions and beer can be rapidly determined by measurements of their refractive indices.

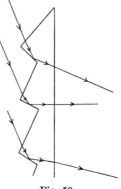

Fig. 50

The method adopted in these cases is a determination of the critical angle which requires a single reading only.

Summary

Laws of refraction.

1. The incident and refracted rays are on opposite sides of, and in the same plane as, the normal.

2. When a ray of light passes from one medium to another the sine of the angle of incidence bears a constant ratio to the sine of the angle of refraction. The ratio is called the refractive index from one medium to the other,

i.e.
$$\mu = \frac{\sin i}{\sin r}.$$

Refraction is caused by a change of velocity as light passes from one medium to another.

A thick glass mirror forms multiple images.

The apparent depth of a block of glass or a pond is less than its true depth owing to refraction. When viewed at right angles to the surface

$$\frac{\text{True depth}}{\text{Apparent depth}} = \mu.$$

When a ray of light passes from a denser to a rarer medium it is totally internally reflected if it makes an angle greater than the critical angle, C, with the normal, where $\sin C = \frac{1}{\mu}$. The phenomenon is exemplified in totally reflecting prisms and the luminous jet.

Refraction occurs in the atmosphere giving rise to phenomena such as the mirage.

On passing through a prism light is deviated. If it suffers minimum deviation D, in a prism of refracting angle A,

$$\mu = \frac{\sin \frac{A+D}{2}}{\sin \frac{A}{2}}.$$

QUESTIONS

When asked to draw refracted rays accurately to scale, use the method explained in Example 1.

1. The following is a geometrical construction for finding the refracted ray when a given incident ray strikes a plane surface separating two media. In Fig. 51 the incident ray *AB* passes from air to glass of refractive index 1·5 or $\frac{3}{2}$.

With centre *B* (the point of incidence) and any convenient radius, describe a circle, cutting the incident ray at *A*. Drop a perpendicular *AM* to the surface of the glass. Divide *BM* into three equal parts and mark off a distance *BN* equal to two of these parts. Erect the perpendicular *NC*. Then *BC* is the refracted ray.

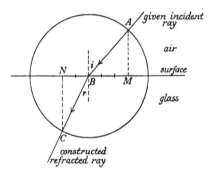

Fig. 51

Make an accurate construction of the refracted ray using an incident ray at an angle of 60° with the normal to the surface. Prove the construction, i.e. show that

$$\mu \left(= \frac{\sin i}{\sin r} \right) = 1\cdot5.$$

2. State the laws of refraction. A ray of light falls on one face of a parallel plate of glass and emerges from the opposite face. Find graphically or otherwise the displacement of the ray if its angle of incidence on the first face is 60°. The thickness of the block is 0·5 cm. and the index of refraction of the glass is 1·5. (O. & C.)

3. A narrow beam of light from an electric lamp under water of refractive index 4/3 strikes the surface. Draw diagrams to scale to

show the direction of the reflected and refracted beams for angles of incidence of 20°, 40°, and 60°. Indicate roughly the relative intensities of the reflected and refracted beams. (C.)

4. Explain why, when placed on the bottom of a deep vessel, a coin, which is just out of sight to an eye situated above and to the side of the vessel, comes into view when the vessel is filled with water.

5. A stick partly immersed in water and inclined to the surface, appears to bend. Draw a diagram showing two rays from the bottom of the stick which, after refraction, enter the eye; and hence explain the appearance of the stick.

6. Define "refractive index". Indicate briefly what you consider to be the cause of the refraction of light.

What is the velocity of light in a diamond, of refractive index 2·4?

(Velocity of light in air = 186,000 m.p.sec.)

7. Explain, with the aid of a diagram, why a pool of water appears to be shallower than it is. Deduce the relation between the real and the apparent depth when the pool is viewed vertically from above. (C.)

8. A transparent cube of 15 cm. edge contains a small air bubble. Its apparent depth when viewed through one face of the cube is 6 cm. and when viewed through the opposite face it is 4 cm. What is the actual distance of the bubble from the first face and what is the refractive index of the substance of the cube? (C.)

9. Explain why a ray of light travelling in water and striking the surface separating water from air at an angle of incidence greater than 49° cannot emerge into the air. (μ for water = 1·33.)

A fish is situated 2 ft. below the surface of a pond. Describe with the help of a careful diagram what it will see in various directions by direct vision and by reflection and refraction at the surface of the water. (C.)

10. Explain the terms *total reflection, critical angle*.

What is the refractive index of a substance whose critical angle is 35°?

11. Under what conditions is light totally reflected at the surface separating two media?

Show, by means of a diagram, how a beam of light may be turned through a right angle by means of an isosceles right-angled glass prism. Explain why the same effect could not be produced with a similar prism made of ice. (Critical angle for glass-air surface = 41°; critical angle for ice-air surface = 50°.) (C.)

12. Explain carefully, with the aid of diagrams:

(*a*) If the light from an electric filament be reflected from a slab of red glass two images are seen, one white and one red.

(*b*) If an iron ball coated with soot from a candle flame is immersed in water in a beaker it appears like polished silver.

(*c*) A stream appears shallower when viewed obliquely from the bank than when viewed vertically from a bridge above.

13. On looking obliquely through the thick glass window of a railway carriage a passenger sees a group of faint images of a distant street lamp which approach closer to each other as the train comes towards the lamp. Explain with the aid of diagrams.

14. "Pools of water" can sometimes be seen on a road, usually at the crest of a slight hill, on a hot sunny day, which disappear on closer inspection. Explain, with a diagram, how they are formed.

15. Explain:

If a candle flame is viewed through a glass prism placed with the refracting edge at the top, the apparent position of the candle is above its true position. (O. & C.)

16. State the laws of refraction of light, illustrating your answer by means of a diagram.

A ray of light strikes the surface of a 60° glass prism at an angle of incidence of 40°. Make an accurate drawing to show the path of the ray through the prism, and measure the angle of deviation. ($\mu = 1 \cdot 5$.)
(O. & C.)

17. Explain what is meant by *critical angle* and *total reflection*. Draw the path of a ray of light which is incident (*a*) at grazing incidence, (*b*) normally, on the face of a glass prism of refractive index $1 \cdot 5$ and refracting angle 60°. What will be the deviation produced in each case? (O. & C.)

18. What do you understand by *refracting angle* of a prism and *angle of deviation*? Show how you would carry out an experiment with a given prism with the object of finding out how the angle of deviation varies with the angle of incidence. What important conclusions would you draw from the results of your experiment? (L.)

19. Define the refractive index of glass, explaining clearly by means of a diagram the terms used.

PQ represents the path of a ray of light passing through an equilateral glass prism (see Fig. 52). *AP* is the incident ray, and *QB* the emergent ray. It is noted that the angle between the directions of *AP* and *QB* is 40°. Draw *AP* and *QB* in their correct positions, and by suitable measurement from your diagram, or otherwise, determine the value of the refractive index of the prism. (sin 50° = 0·766.)

(L.)

20. Explain, with the aid of a diagram, how underground rooms may be lighted by glass prisms let into the pavement above.

(O. & C.)

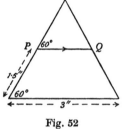

Fig. 52

21. A beam of light from a distant source falls upon the surface of a solid cylindrical block of glass whose axis is at right angles to the direction of the beam. Trace the course of a single ray which does not pass through the axis. Under what circumstances would a pencil undergo no deviation whatever on passing through the glass? ($\mu = 1·5$.)

(N.)

Chapter IV

LENSES

A thin piece of glass, having one or both of its faces appropriately curved, has a remarkable property: it can direct light entering it from any one point on an object to another point on the other side of it and can thus form an image of the entire object on a screen. Such a piece of glass is called a lens. The lens of a camera, for example, throws a sharp image on the photographic plate and the projector lens of a lantern forms a magnified image of a lantern slide on a screen.

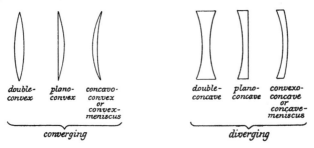

Fig. 53

The lens, so called because of its similarity in shape to a lentil seed, was known to the ancient Greeks. But, for hundreds of thousands of years before this, lenses had been made by Nature in the eyes of most living creatures. We shall study in the next chapter the action of the lens in the human eye.

Types of lenses.

Lenses are of two main types, *converging* (or convex) and *diverging* (or concave). The former cause light to converge (see Plate III, facing p. 64) and are always thicker in the middle than at the edge: the latter cause light to diverge and are thinner in the middle than at the edge. Fig. 53 shows different forms of these two general types of lenses.

Terms used in connection with lenses.

A simple type of lens possesses two spherical surfaces. The centres of the spheres of which the surfaces are part are called the centres of curvature of the surfaces. The line joining the centres of curvature is called the *principal axis* of the lens. The point O (see Fig. 54) on the *principal axis* of a lens midway between its two surfaces is called the *optical centre*. The "width" or diameter, AB, is called the *aperture* of the lens. The plane through O, perpendicular to the principal axis (of which AB is a section), is called the *principal plane*. In our treatment of lenses we shall consider only thin lenses, and regard them, for the purpose of drawing rays, as consisting only of a principal plane.

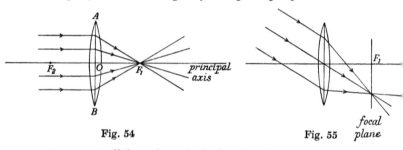

Fig. 54   Fig. 55   focal plane

All rays parallel to the principal axis of a converging lens of small aperture are refracted through a point F_1 (see Fig. 54), called the *principal focus*. The distance OF_1 is called the *focal length* of the lens. A lens has two principal foci (F_1 and F_2 in Fig. 54), since light may be incident on either side: $OF_2 = OF_1$.

A parallel beam of light, inclined to the principal axis of a converging lens, is refracted through a point in a plane through F_1 perpendicular to the principal axis, called the *focal plane* (see Fig. 55).

When a beam of light, parallel to the principal axis, falls on a diverging lens, it is caused to diverge as though proceeding from the *principal focus*, F_1 (see Fig. 56). F_2 is the other principal focus. The same terms apply to a diverging as to a converging lens.

In Figs. 54 and 56 rays have been drawn straight up to the principal planes of the lenses and there caused to bend suddenly. This is convenient for construction purposes but is not a true picture of what is actually happening.

A lens may be regarded as made up of a large number of prisms. In Fig. 57 a converging and a diverging lens are considered for simplicity as consisting of several prisms. Light, on entering each prism, is bent towards the normal and, on leaving, away from the normal. This shows the kind of path actually taken by light inside a lens.

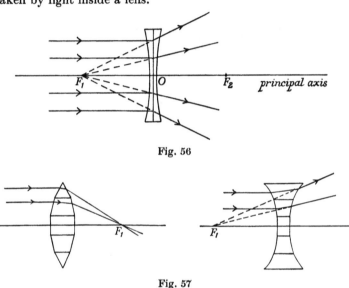

Fig. 56

Fig. 57

Graphical construction of the image formed by a lens.

An image of a bright object such as a window may be focused by means of a converging lens on a sheet of paper. It is possible to predict the size and position of the image if the focal length of the lens and also the distance of the object from the lens are known.

This may be done graphically by drawing two rays from the top of the object:

1. *A ray parallel to the principal axis which is refracted through the principal focus of the lens;*

2. *A ray through the optical centre of the lens, which passes through undeviated.*

(A third ray is sometimes convenient, i.e. a ray from the top of the object passing through or approaching F_2 which is refracted so as to emerge parallel to the axis.)

An explanation of the behaviour of the second ray is necessary. A lens, at its middle, may be regarded as a parallel-sided slab of glass. Now we have seen, in Chapter III, that a ray after passing through a parallel-sided slab of glass emerges parallel to its original direction, but displaced laterally. If the lens is very thin the lateral displacement can be ignored, and the ray may be regarded as proceeding straight through.

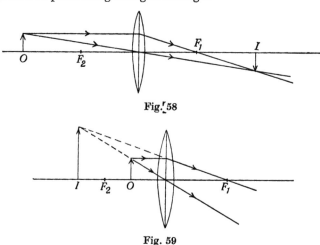

Fig. 58

Fig. 59

Images formed by a converging lens.

A converging lens can form images of two types:

1. It forms a *real* image when the object is at a greater distance from the lens than its focal length (see Fig. 58). This image is always inverted and may be diminished or magnified. We may subdivide the cases when a real image is formed as follows:

Let u = distance of object from lens,

f = focal length of lens.

(a) When $u > 2f$, image is diminished.
(b) When $u = 2f$, image is same size as object.
(c) When $u < 2f$, image is magnified.

The student should draw all these cases for himself.

2. It forms a *virtual* image when the object is at a shorter distance from the lens than its focal length (see Fig. 59). This image is always erect and magnified. It cannot be thrown on to a screen, since the virtual rays forming it have no physical existence, and are therefore dotted in the figure.

Images formed by a diverging lens.

A diverging lens always forms a virtual, erect and diminished image of a real object (see Fig. 60).

Conjugate points.

Since rays of light are reversible in direction, object and real image are interchangeable. Such points as O and I in Figs. 58, 59 and 60, are called *conjugate points*, or conjugate foci. (Why are not object and virtual image interchangeable?)

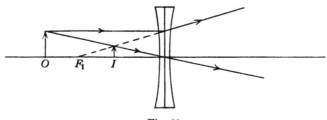

Fig. 60

Calculation of the position of the image.

In Fig. 61 let f, u and v stand for the focal length of the lens, and the distances of the object and image from the lens respectively. There is a relation between these quantities, $\dfrac{1}{u}+\dfrac{1}{v}=\dfrac{1}{f}$, which we will now prove.

$\triangle$s JIC and QOC are similar.

$$\therefore \quad \frac{JI}{QO}=\frac{CI}{CO}=\frac{v}{u}.$$

$\triangle$s JIF_1 and ACF_1 are similar.

$$\therefore \quad \frac{JI}{AC}=\frac{IF_1}{CF_1}=\frac{v-f}{f}.$$

But $AC = QO$ since QA is parallel to OC.

$$\therefore \; \frac{JI}{QO} = \frac{v}{u} = \frac{v-f}{f}.$$

$$\therefore \; vf = uv - uf.$$

Divide both sides by uvf.

$$\frac{1}{u} = \frac{1}{f} - \frac{1}{v},$$

i.e.

$$\frac{1}{u} + \frac{1}{v} = \frac{1}{f}.$$

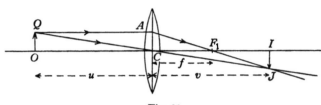

Fig. 61

Using Fig. 59 we can derive in a similar manner,

$$\frac{1}{u} - \frac{1}{v} = \frac{1}{f}.$$

Using Fig. 60 we can derive

$$\frac{1}{u} - \frac{1}{v} = -\frac{1}{f}.$$

The student should verify these last two cases, which differ from the previous case in respect of the algebraic signs.

The sign convention.

By using a sign convention, one formula

$$\frac{1}{u} + \frac{1}{v} = \frac{1}{f}$$

can be made to fit all three cases.

Distances actually travelled by the light are taken as positive, and distances measured along a virtual ray as negative. Thus the distances from a real object to a lens and from a lens to a real image are always positive, whereas the distance from a lens to a virtual image is negative. (Remember that the distances u, v, f are taken along the principal axis.)

The focal length of a converging lens is positive (OF_1 in Fig. 54).

The focal length of a diverging lens is negative (OF_1 in Fig. 56).

In Fig. 61 all three quantities u, v, f have the same sign: they are positive. Hence the formula obtained is the correct one,

$$\frac{1}{u}+\frac{1}{v}=\frac{1}{f}.$$

In Fig. 59, f is positive, v is negative and u is positive. When no regard is paid to algebraic signs, the formula $\frac{1}{u}-\frac{1}{v}=\frac{1}{f}$ is obtained. Allowing for the signs the formula becomes $\frac{1}{u}+\frac{1}{v}=\frac{1}{f}$.

Again in Fig. 60, f and v are negative and u is positive. The formula obtained using no sign convention is $\frac{1}{u}-\frac{1}{v}=-\frac{1}{f}$. Allowing for the signs, the formula becomes $\frac{1}{u}+\frac{1}{v}=\frac{1}{f}$.

Thus the one formula, $\frac{1}{u}+\frac{1}{v}=\frac{1}{f}$, may be used for all cases if the sign convention is properly observed, i.e. if the numerical values of u, v and f are given their correct sign when substituting in the formula.

Magnification.

A lens which forms an image twice as high as the object is said to produce a magnification of 2.

Definition.

$$\textbf{Magnification} = \frac{\textbf{Height of image}}{\textbf{Height of object}}.$$

(In the case of an ordinary lens with spherical surfaces, the width and every other dimension perpendicular to the axis are magnified in the same ratio as the height.)

It can be shown very simply that

$$\textbf{Magnification} = \frac{\textbf{v}}{\textbf{u}}.$$

In Fig. 61 since the $\triangle$s JIC and QOC are similar,

$$\text{Magnification} = \frac{QO}{JI} = \frac{CI}{CO} = \frac{v}{u}.$$

Example. An object 2·5 cm. high is placed 15 cm. from and perpendicular to the axis of a converging lens of focal length 20 cm. Find the position and height of the image.

In the formula
$$\frac{1}{u} + \frac{1}{v} = \frac{1}{f}$$

$$u = +15 \text{ cm.} \quad \text{and} \quad f = +20 \text{ cm.}$$

$$\frac{1}{15} + \frac{1}{v} = \frac{1}{20},$$

$$\frac{1}{v} = \frac{1}{20} - \frac{1}{15}$$

$$= -\frac{1}{60},$$

$$v = -60 \text{ cm.}$$

Hence the image is 60 cm. in front of the lens and virtual.

Now
$$\frac{\text{Height of image}}{\text{Height of object}} = \frac{v}{u},$$

$$\frac{\text{Height of image}}{2·5} = \frac{60}{15},$$

$$\text{Height of image} = \frac{60 \times 2·5}{15}$$

$$= 10 \text{ cm.}$$

The student should check this result by making a drawing accurately to scale.

Spherical aberration.

The simple lens suffers from a number of defects, all of which must be corrected before a perfectly focused, undistorted image can be formed. The correction is usually accomplished by combining a number of lenses, some of which are cemented together.

PLATE III

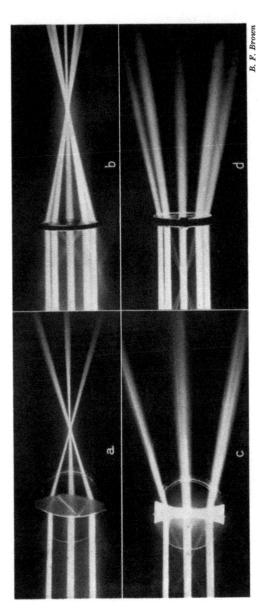

B. F. Brown

Photographs of light passing through lenses: (a) a sectional (or cylindrical) converging lens, (b) an ordinary, spherical converging lens, (c) a sectional diverging lens, and (d) a spherical diverging lens. Note that the lenses render each separate beam converging or diverging. Note also the internal reflections inside the lens in (a), the reflection from the inside concave face in (b), the reflections from the first concave faces in (c) and (d). The luminous rings round the lenses in (a) and (c) are the holders to which the lenses are attached. The beams were rendered visible by means of smoke in a smoke box.

PLATE IV

D. G. A. Dyson

(a)

Refraction of water waves. The straight white lines, drawn on the photograph at right angles to the wave fronts, represent rays. The refraction is due to a reduction in the velocity of the waves as they pass from deeper to shallower water.

D. G. A

(b)   *(c)*

Water waves passing through a converging lens. In *(b)* the source of the waves is at the principal focus of the lens and the emergent waves are straight —corresponding to a parallel beam. In *(c)* the emergent waves converge to a focus (the image of the source), and diverge again. The water lens is formed by placing a piece of glass shaped like a lens but of uniform thickness, on the floor of the ripple tank. The waves travel more slowly above this piece of glass, since the water is shallower.

Only one defect can be mentioned here, spherical aberration. Rays of light parallel to the axis and falling on a lens of large aperture are not all refracted through the principal focus. The refracted rays do not pass through a point but envelope a caustic (see also p. 102). Thus when using a cheap uncorrected camera lens, unless a very small aperture is employed—necessitating a long exposure—the image cannot be perfectly focused.

Demonstration of the action of a lens on the wave theory.

No special explanation of the action of a lens on the corpuscular theory is necessary since the corpuscles may be assumed to follow the paths of the rays already described. The explanation on the wave theory, however, is not so straightforward.

Plate IV (*b*) and (*c*), opposite, are photographs of water waves passing through converging lenses. A flat sheet of glass of uniform thickness with curved sides (i.e. shaped like a lens) is placed in a ripple tank. The water above the lens is shallower than in the rest of the tank, and hence the velocity of the waves above the lens is reduced. Note how the lenses change the curvature of the waves.

Power of a lens.

The shorter the focal length of a lens the more does it cause rays to bend. The "power" of a lens is defined as $\frac{1}{\text{Focal length}}$. Thus if a diverging lens is placed in contact with a converging lens of greater power, i.e. of shorter focal length, the combination will be converging. If the focal length of the diverging lens is the shorter, i.e. it has the greater power, the combination is diverging.

The power of a lens is measured in dioptres. A lens having a focal length of 1 metre is said to have a power of 1 dioptre. Thus

$$\text{Power of lens in dioptres} = \frac{1}{\text{Focal length in metres}}.$$

Now the curvature of a spherical wave is defined as

$$\frac{1}{\text{Radius in metres}}.$$

Thus if u and v metres are the distances of a point object and image from a lens, the curvature of the incident and emergent waves at the lens are $\dfrac{1}{u}$ and $\dfrac{1}{v}$. The formula $\dfrac{1}{u}+\dfrac{1}{v}=\dfrac{1}{f}$ therefore assumes a new significance.

If we write it

$$\frac{1}{v}=\frac{1}{f}-\frac{1}{u},$$

its meaning becomes

Curvature of emergent wave =
    Power of lens – Curvature of incident wave.

Opticians always classify spectacle lenses by their powers in dioptres, instead of using their focal lengths.

Two thin lenses in contact.

If two thin lenses (focal lengths f_1 and f_2) are placed in contact the focal length of the combination f is given by the formula

$$\frac{1}{f}=\frac{1}{f_1}+\frac{1}{f_2}.$$

In other words, the power of the combination is equal to the sum of the powers of the two constituent lenses (i.e. $F=F_1+F_2$).

A convenient method of finding the focal length of a diverging lens is to combine it with a converging lens of greater power (i.e. shorter focal length), when the combination is converging. The focal lengths of the combination and also of the converging lens alone are found by one of the methods given on pp. 68–73: hence the focal length of the diverging lens may be calculated from the formula given above.

Manufacture of lenses.

The manufacture of high-class lenses to be used, for example, in photographic cameras, is a long and expensive process.

Glass is made by fusing together quartz, sand, soda and lime. The glass may be given different optical properties by adding salts of sodium, barium and lead. The melting pots are made of alumina and (in a particular instance) are 5 ft. in diameter: they hold 2 tons of glass*. They are heated to a temperature of 1500° C. for 18 hours, and are stirred with a bar of alumina to enable the liberated gases to escape. They are then withdrawn

* See *Photographic Lenses*, Carl Zeiss.

from the fire and allowed to cool in another furnace very slowly for a week. Even at this slow rate of cooling the mass of glass cracks into a large number of irregular lumps (see Fig. 62). These are broken away with a hammer and then each is melted down again in a rectangular fire-clay mould until the glass becomes viscous. The cooling on this occasion requires a month, possibly three months, in order to minimise the possibility of

By courtesy of Messrs Carl Zeiss

Fig. 62. A cooled pot with cracked raw glass.

internal strains. When cold all the glass is tested very carefully for internal strains, and on the average 85 per cent. of the original glass is rejected as unfit for optical purposes and sold to manufacturers of ordinary glassware.

A small piece of a glass slab which has passed the tests is cut off and shaped into the form of a prism, which is used to find the refractive index and other optical constants of the glass.

From these determinations mathematicians calculate the necessary curvature of the lens faces.

The grinding tools, consisting of shallow cups of iron or brass
with the reverse curvature of the lens, are then made with great
precision on a lathe. For a convex lens surface a concave tool is
required, and for a concave lens surface, a mushroom-like tool
(see Fig. 63).

The glass, before grinding, is sawn into rough shape by a
special circular saw, consisting of an iron disc having a rim of
fine diamond splinters (see Fig. 64).

In the process of grinding, the glass is attached to a rotating
spindle and pressed against the tool, in which is placed an
abrading material of emery and water (see Fig. 65). As the
lens takes shape the abrading material is made finer and finer,
and the final polish is obtained by using jeweller's rouge.

The lens is then tested, cemented to other lenses if necessary,
centred and mounted (great care being necessary to ensure that
the axes of all the lenses coincide). Finally it is subjected to
further rigorous tests including the photographing of a test
chart (see Fig. 66).

EXPERIMENTS WITH LENSES

EXPERIMENT 1. *To verify the formulae*

$$(a)\ \frac{1}{u}+\frac{1}{v}=\frac{1}{f}, \qquad (b)\ Magnification=\frac{v}{u},$$

for a converging lens.

For this experiment a luminous object is required. A piece of
frosted glass on which is painted a pair of black crossed lines, illuminated from behind by an electric lamp, is suitable.

Place this object, O, on the axis of the converging lens, held
vertically (see that the centre of the lens is at the same height as the
middle of the crossed lines), and focus the image, I, as sharply as
possible on a white screen by adjusting the position of the screen (see
Fig. 58). Measure u and v and hence calculate f using the formula

$$\frac{1}{u}+\frac{1}{v}=\frac{1}{f}.$$

Obtain a series of pairs of values of u and v (with the values of u as
widely ranged as possible) and calculate f in each case. If the formula
is correct, the values of f should be constant.

Fig. 63. Grinding tools with lenses.

Fig. 64. Cutting the glass slabs.

Fig. 65. Polishing the lenses.

Fig. 66. Testing laboratory for photographic lenses.

Measure also the height (or one of the dimensions) of the object and of each image. Calculate in each case

$$\frac{\text{Height of image}}{\text{Height of object}} \quad \text{and} \quad \frac{v}{u}.$$

Hence verify the formula

$$\text{Magnification} = \frac{v}{u}.$$

Results should be set out in the form of a table.

EXPERIMENT 2. *To find the focal length f of a converging lens, using*

(a) *a rough focusing method,* (b) *two pins (or triangular paper flags),*
(c) *a plane mirror and a pin.*

(a) A rough determination of f may be made by focusing the image of a distant window on to a sheet of paper. The distance between the lens and the paper is approximately equal to f since the object may be considered to be at infinity, and therefore rays of light which enter the lens from any one point on the object are nearly parallel to one another.

(b) Place a pin on one side of and perpendicular to the axis of the converging lens, adjust the position of another pin on the other side of the lens so that there is no parallax between it and the real image of the first pin (see Fig. 57). Measure u and v and hence calculate f from the formula

$$\frac{1}{u} + \frac{1}{v} = \frac{1}{f}.$$

The method is similar to that of Experiment 1: a pin-parallax method is, however, more accurate than a focusing method. Several values of u and v should be taken.

The object pin O should be well illuminated and hence it is desirable for the experimenter, who looks through the lens from behind I, to have his back to a window. The light from the window will then shine on that side of the pin which faces the lens. Again the height of the pins should be adjusted so that the tip of the one appears just to touch the tip of the image of the other. Then a very slight relative movement of pin and image, on moving the head, may be detected. Even when accurately adjusted, however, the pin and the image will keep together only when they appear in the middle of the lens. There is bound to be relative movement between them near the periphery of the lens owing to spherical aberration (see p. 64). When adjusting the second pin remember that if it moves in the same direction as the eye it is further away from the eye than the image and *vice versa* (see also description of Plate VII, below).

Remember also, that in order that a converging lens may form a real image, the object must be at a greater distance from the lens than f, and also the distance between the object and image must be at least $4f$.

(*c*) Place a plane mirror on one side of the converging lens, and at right angles to the axis of the lens (see Fig. 67). Adjust the position of a pin on the other side of the lens, and perpendicular to the axis so

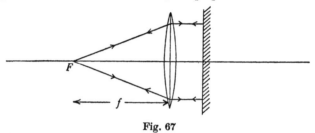

Fig. 67

that there is no parallax between it and its image as seen on looking into the lens. The distance of the pin from the lens is then equal to f. Why? Take several readings.

Plate VII, facing p. 128, illustrates the no-parallax adjustment in this experiment.

EXPERIMENT 3. *To find the focal length of a diverging lens.*

A diverging lens always forms a virtual image of a real object on the same side of the lens as the object. Since the image is virtual the focusing method is impossible and since the image is formed on the far side as one looks through the lens, the pin-parallax method is difficult and inaccurate.

(*a*) Try the ordinary pin-parallax method (similar to Experiment 2*b*) and see how consistent are your results. Place a pin in front of the lens and another large pin, the top of which may be seen above the lens, on the same side. Adjust this second pin so that there is no parallax between the top of it (as seen over the lens) and the image of the other pin. Measure u and v and calculate f.

(*b*) The method can be made more accurate by the following modification.

Place a pin O in front of the lens (see Fig. 68). The image will be formed at some point I. Place a plane mirror M and a pin A on the other side of the lens, and move A until its image in M coincides with the image of O formed by the lens: the images formed by both lens and mirror are then at I.

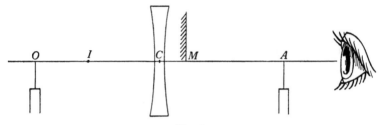

Fig. 68

To calculate f, use the formula

$$\frac{1}{u}+\frac{1}{v}=\frac{1}{f}.$$

$$v = -CI = -(MI-MC)$$
$$= -(AM-MC),$$

since $\qquad AM = MI.$

Hence, measure AM, MC, CO.

SUMMARY

There are two main types of lenses, converging and diverging.

The position and size of the image formed by a thin lens of small aperture may be determined by the formulae

$$\frac{1}{u}+\frac{1}{v}=\frac{1}{f},$$

$$\text{Magnification} = \frac{\text{Height of image}}{\text{Height of object}} = \frac{v}{u},$$

where $u =$ distance from object to lens, $v =$ distance from lens to image, $f =$ distance from lens to principal focus, i.e. the focal length.

Distances actually travelled by the light are taken as positive, and distances measured along a virtual ray are taken as negative. The focal length of a converging lens is positive, and of a diverging lens, negative.

Power of a lens in dioptres $= \dfrac{1}{\text{Focal length (in metres)}}.$

Experimental determination of the focal length of a lens.

1. *Converging lens.*

(*a*) Rough focusing method using distant window as object. Image is at principal focus.

(*b*) Determination of *u* and *v* using luminous object and focusing method. Then $\dfrac{1}{u}+\dfrac{1}{v}=\dfrac{1}{f}$.

(*c*) Determination of *u* and *v* by pin-parallax method.

(*d*) Plane mirror behind lens: image coincides in position with object at the principal focus. Focusing *or* pin-parallax method.

2. *Diverging lens.*

The determination of the focal length is difficult because the image is virtual and is on the same side of the lens as the object.

(*a*) Rough pin-parallax method using distant object when image is at the principal focus.

(*b*) Use plane mirror and pin-parallax method. (This method is quite different from Exp. 1 (*d*).)

(*c*) Combine with converging lens of greater power,

$$\frac{1}{f}=\frac{1}{f_1}+\frac{1}{f_2}.$$

QUESTIONS

Draw rough ray diagrams wherever possible in order to check that your calculation is approximately correct, and also to illustrate your answer.

1. Find by calculation and also by *accurate* drawing the position, height and nature of the image formed by a converging lens of focal length 1 in. when an object 0·6 in. high is placed (*a*) 1·5 in., (*b*) 0·8 in., from it.

2. Find by calculation and accurate drawing the position, height and nature of the image formed by a diverging lens of focal length 5 cm. when an object 3 cm. high is placed 10 cm. from it.

3. (a) How would you test whether a spectacle lens, of low power, is converging or diverging?

(b) What is the difference between a real and a virtual image? Is a virtual object possible?

(c) Why does a diverging lens always produce a diminished image?

4. State fully for what positions of the object a converging lens forms (a) real, (b) virtual, (c) magnified, (d) diminished, (e) erect, (f) inverted, images.

5. A camera with a lens of focal length 20 cm. is used to photograph an object 200 cm. from the lens. How far must the plate be from the lens and how will the size of the image compare with the size of the object? (O.)

6. An object, 10 in. in front of a lens, forms an image 3 in. from the lens on the same side. Is the lens converging or diverging and what is its focal length?

7. Derive an expression connecting the focal length of a thin lens with the distances of the object and image from the lens.

A lantern slide 3 in. square is to be projected so as to give an image 8 ft. square on a screen 30 ft. away. What should be the focal length of the lens required? (O. & C.)

8. A camera is often provided with a scale on which are marked the positions at which the lens must be placed for photographing objects at 6, 10, 30 and 100 ft. and infinity, respectively. Draw a plan of the scale for a lens of 3 in. focal length. (O. & C.)

9. Explain the meaning of (a) the principal focus of a lens, (b) the image of an object.

A candle is 1 metre from a screen. It is found that a convex lens placed 20 cm. from the candle throws a sharp image on the screen. In what other place can the lens be put so as to cast a sharp image on the screen? Calculate the focal length of the lens. (C.)

10. A luminous object and a screen are 1 metre apart. A convex lens placed between them produces an image on the screen three times the size of the object. What is the focal length of the lens?

A second position of the lens also gives an image on the screen; what is this position and what is the size of the image? (L.)

11. What is meant by the focal length of a lens?

Calculate at what distance from a converging lens of focal length 20 cm. an object must be placed in order that the image may be (a) real, and three times the size of the object; (b) virtual, and three times the size of the object.

Draw diagrams to illustrate the two cases.   (O. & C.)

12. Draw diagrams to illustrate how a convex lens may produce a magnified image (a) which is real, (b) which is virtual.

A convex lens situated 6 in. from an object produces a real image four times the size of the object. Where must the lens be placed to give a virtual image three times the size of the object?   (C.)

13. Illustrate, with the aid of diagrams, that a converging lens cannot form a real image on a screen which is distant less than 4f from the object. (Take an object at a distance from the lens of (i) ∞ , (ii) 2f, (iii) f.)

14. A bi-convex lens 3 cm. thick has faces of radii of curvature 10 cm. and 15 cm. respectively. Trace, on a good-sized diagram, the course of a ray of light which comes from a point source placed on the axis of the lens 20 cm. in front of the face of smaller radius of curvature and passes through the lens. The refractive index of the glass is 1·5. Explain your construction.   (O. & C.)

15. A convex lens has a small object placed on its axis distant from a focal point by an amount equal to one-quarter of the focal length. Prove that the image has linear dimensions four times as great as the object. Distinguish between the two possible cases.

(N.)

16. A camera has a lens of focal length 5 in., and takes a photograph $3\frac{1}{2} \times 2\frac{1}{2}$ in. In order to take as large a full-length photograph as possible of a 6 ft. man, how far away from the man must the camera be placed?

17. If you wished to throw on a wall a magnified image of a brightly illuminated object lying flat on a table, how could you do so with the aid of a lens and a plane mirror?

Show further the exact positions you would adopt to get the image magnified four times in diameter, using a lens of 2 ft. focus.   (N.)

18. An object 1 cm. in height is placed at a distance of 10 metres from a screen. A lens is used to form on the screen an image of height 19 cm. What kind of lens must be used, where must it be placed, and what must be its focal length?   (O. & C.)

19. Explain what is meant by the principal axis, optical centre, and principal focus of a lens.

Light is converging to a point P, and a convex lens of focal length 20 cm. is placed at A in the path of the beam, where $AP = 30$ cm. The beam now converges to Q. Calculate the distance AQ.   (L.)

20. State the formula connecting the distance of an object and its image from a lens with the magnification.

Describe an experiment by which this formula can be verified for a convex lens.

The sun is 9.3×10^7 miles from the earth, and it is found that a lens of focal length 10 in. gives an image of the sun 0·0935 in. in diameter. What is the diameter of the sun?   (O.)

21. A point source of light is placed 12 in. from a converging lens of diameter 2 in. and focal length 6 in. What is the diameter of the patch of light which the lens throws upon a wall, situated 6 in. from it on the other side of the source?

22. The image of an object on the axis of a convex lens is formed on a screen 80 cm. from the object. On moving the lens 15 cm. along the axis another image of the same object is formed on the same screen. What is the focal length of the lens?   (L.)

23. When a convex lens is placed above an empty tank an image of a mark on the bottom of the tank, which is 45 cm. from the lens, is formed 36 cm. above the lens. When a liquid is poured into the tank to a depth of 40 cm. the distance of the image of the mark above the lens is 48 cm. Find the refractive index of the liquid.

(C., 1st M.B.)

24. The sun subtends an angle of $\frac{1}{2}°$ (approx.) at the earth. What is the diameter of the sun's image formed by a converging lens of focal length 3 ft.?

25. A convex lens of 10 cm. focal length is used to form an image of an object. Plot a curve showing the relation between the magnification and the distance of the image from the lens as the object is taken at different distances from the lens.   (L.)

26. How would you set to work if you were given two thin lenses, one convex, the other concave, and were asked to find their focal lengths?   (N.)

27.   There are two co-axial lenses, 6 cm. apart, one is a converging lens of focal length 2·5 cm. and the other a diverging lens of focal length 3 cm. An object 1 cm. high is placed perpendicular to the axis 5 cm. beyond the converging lens. Find both by calculation and accurate drawing the position and height of the final image formed. (Find the image formed by the converging lens: treat this as an ordinary object in front of the diverging lens.)

28.   Two co-axial converging lenses, each of focal length 1 in., are placed 3 in. apart. An object 0·4 in. high is placed 1·25 in. in front of one of these lenses. Calculate the position and height of the final image. Try to devise a method of solving this problem by drawing.

Chapter V

SIMPLE OPTICAL INSTRUMENTS

The photographic camera.

The photographic camera consists of a light-tight box, having a converging lens at the front which throws a real image on to a sensitive plate or film at the back.

The plate is coated with gelatine impregnated with a silver salt and under the action of light the salt undergoes a peculiar change. Those parts which have been acted on by light readily become reduced to black finely-divided silver on treatment with a suitable reducing agent termed a developer. The unaltered silver salt is then removed by a fixing solution to prevent further action of light. The process is completed by washing and drying. The resulting image is clearly a "negative" since the dark parts are those corresponding with the bright parts of the image originally formed by the camera lens.

In order to focus objects at different distances from the camera the lens is often attached to bellows so that it may be moved towards or away from the plate. However, in a box camera, no such provision usually is made for the movement of the lens. By using a lens of short focal length (about $3\frac{1}{2}$ in.) and small aperture, it is possible to bring to an approximate focus on the plate the images of all objects at a greater distance from the camera than about 6 ft.

Cameras with bellows are equipped with a variable diaphragm or stop behind the lens, which enables the aperture to be varied. A small indicator enables the diameter of the stop to be adjusted as a rule to the following fractions of the focal length: $f/32, f/22, f/16, f/11, f/8, f/5\cdot6, f/4\cdot5$.

Now the area of the stop is proportional to the square of the diameter. If the values $\dfrac{1}{32^2}, \dfrac{1}{22^2}, \dfrac{1}{16^2}, \dfrac{1}{11^2}$, etc. are worked out they will be found to be approximately in the ratio $1 : 2 : 4 : 8$, etc. Hence, the amount of light admitted into the camera with these different stops varies in the same ratio, and thus twice the exposure is necessary at $f/32$ as at $f/22$.

When using a small stop a longer exposure is required than with a large one, but the advantage gained is a greater "depth of focus". The depth of focus is the distance between the nearest and furthest objects which are just sufficiently in focus to look reasonably clear in the print.

Fig. 69 illustrates how depth of focus may be increased by reducing the aperture of a lens. The lens forms an image of the top point P of an object, at A. When the plate is in the position shown the image of P on the plate is not a point but a circular patch BC. If the stop is reduced the diameter of this circular patch (now formed by the dotted lines in the figure) is also reduced. So long as the diameter of the circular patch is less than

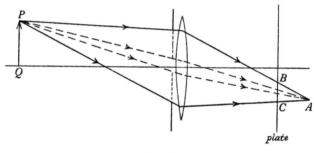

Fig. 69

$\frac{1}{100}$th in. the image of P formed on the plate is sufficiently in focus for practical purposes unless big enlargements are to be made from the negative. Thus with a small stop the image of P is sufficiently in focus on the plate; with a large stop it is not.

The optical lantern.

The optical lantern is similar in principle to a camera with the object and image interchanged. A large real image of a lantern slide is thrown upon a distant screen by means of a converging lens (or system of lenses) called the projector. Since the image is inverted, the lantern slide is put into its carrier upside down.

Intense illumination of the lantern slide is necessary since the image is so much magnified and consequently very much less

bright. The lantern slide is therefore illuminated by an arc light
or powerful lamp, and a converging lens, called the condenser,
causes the light to converge upon the slide (see Fig. 70).

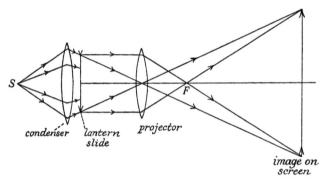

Fig. 70. The optical lantern.

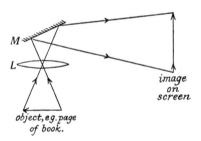

Fig. 71. The epidiascope.

The epidiascope.

Fig. 71 represents the optical arrangement of an epidiascope,
a lantern for projecting on a screen a magnified image of, for
example, the page of a book. The page is intensely illuminated
by a powerful lamp and special reflectors (not shown in the
figure). A converging lens, *L*, forms a real image of the page and
the light is reflected through approximately 90° by a plane
mirror, *M*, silvered, to eliminate multiple reflections, on the
front.

The eye.

The human eye is like a tiny camera. It consists, essentially, of a converging lens which throws a real image on a sensitive "plate" at the back of the eye (see Fig. 72).

The whole optical system is contained in a small ball, about 1 in. in diameter, called the eyeball. The eyeball is fitted in a socket in the skull, in which it can be made to roll by means of muscles. Since it extends back inside the head only part of the front of it can be seen. Its roundness can be felt by the finger.

Fig. 73 is a diagram of the eyeball. The outer covering is a tough opaque white substance called the *sclerotic*. Part of it, "the white of the eye", is visible.

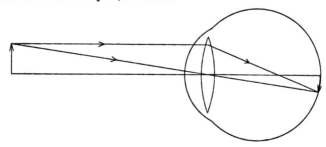

Fig. 72

The eyeball is not perfectly spherical: there is a circular bulge in front of the coloured part, where the sclerotic merges into a transparent, horny, and very tough coating called the *cornea*.

Obtain a small mirror and look at one of your eyes. Notice that the cornea is shiny and reflects like glass.

Behind the cornea is a coloured diaphragm called the *iris* with a circular hole in the middle, called the *pupil*. It is to the colour of the iris that we refer when speaking of the colour of a person's eyes.

The pupil looks black because the inside of the eye is coated with a black pigment (like a camera), called the *choroid*, to prevent internal reflection and consequent fogging of the image. In the eyes of albinos and white rabbits there is no choroid and the pupils have a pink colour, due to the blood in the fine blood vessels at the back of the eye.

The iris corresponds to the stop in a camera. In bright sunlight the pupils contract to reduce the amount of light admitted into the eye; at night the pupil dilates to admit as much light as possible. The phenomenon is most striking in the eyes of certain animals, such as the cat, whose pupils are not circular but slit-like. Look at the image of the pupil of your eye in a small mirror

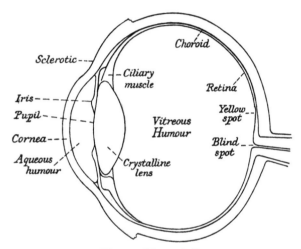

Fig. 73. The eyeball.

Pupil by day   Pupil by night

Fig. 74

with your back to a window. Then turn towards the window and watch the pupil contract (see Fig. 74). This contraction and dilation of the pupil is a reflex action over which we have no control, although by the use of drugs, such as atropine, the oculist may dilate the pupil temporarily to assist examination of the eye and its defects.

Behind the pupil is the *crystalline lens*, made of a jelly-like substance. The curvature of its front face is considerably less than the back face, and it is made up of numerous concentric layers, increasing in density towards the middle. Both these features of the lens tend to diminish spherical aberration.

In order to focus objects at different distances on the plate of a camera, the camera lens has to be moved slightly. There is no such mechanism in the eye. Instead, the focal length of the crystalline lens is changed by the action of muscles, called the *ciliary muscles*, causing it to bulge. When in repose the normal healthy eye is focused for infinity, and the crystalline lens is at its thinnest. The bulging of the lens to focus near objects is called *accommodation*. The power of accommodation is not possessed by children at birth, and it also decreases with age.

The sensitive nerve "plate" at the back of the eye on which the image falls is called the *retina*. It consists of nerve endings, shaped like rods and cones, which are stimulated by light. At the tips of the nerves there is a coloured substance called the *visual purple* which is bleached by light and continually re-generated. The bleaching of the visual purple seems to be an essential part of the act of vision and the sensation caused by it is carried along the *optic nerve* to the brain. In bright sunlight there is comparatively little visual purple in the eye and it is therefore bleached at a slow rate. When we enter a darkened room such as a cinema, it takes some minutes for our eyes to become accustomed to the darkness. During this period a larger quantity of the visual purple is manufactured on the retina, thereby increasing the sensitivity of the eye by as much as a million times.

Between the cornea and the crystalline lens there is a weak salt solution called the *aqueous humour*. Between the aqueous humour and the retina there is a jelly-like substance called the *vitreous humour*. These substances together with the crystalline lens form a compound lens system and make the eye approximately achromatic (see p. 118).

The retina is not equally sensitive all over. Its most sensitive part is in the neighbourhood of a small area, coloured yellow and called the *yellow spot*, which lies on the axis of the crystalline lens. An object which is being viewed is automatically focused on the yellow spot. Besides man, only the monkey (among the mammals) possesses a yellow spot on the retina.

Where the optic nerve divides is the *blind spot*, a part of the retina which is insensitive to light. Since the optic nerve leaves

each eye on the side nearer to the nose, the images in both eyes
never fall simultaneously on the blind spots. The existence of
the blind spot can be demonstrated as follows. Close one eye,
say the left eye, and look at the cross in Fig. 75 with the right
eye. Although one is not looking directly at it, the black circle is
also visible. Move the book towards the eye, and at a certain
distance the black circle seems to disappear. Its image has fallen
on the blind spot. (The cross is focused on the yellow spot, and
since the image is reversed, the black circle is focused on a point
nearer the nose than the yellow spot.) If possible, the student
should obtain a bullock's eye (which is a large eye) from a butcher
and dissect it.

Fig. 75

Vision.

In Fig. 72, for simplicity, all refraction is assumed to take
place at the crystalline lens. Actually, however, there is greater
refraction at the cornea than the lens. Thus under water the eye
cannot focus objects clearly, since light on passing through the
cornea from water is not sufficiently bent.

The image on the retina is upside down and laterally inverted,
but the brain is used from birth to interpreting this correctly.

The crystalline lens is sometimes removed, by an operation,
from an eye suffering from cataract. This disease causes the
crystalline lens to become hard and opaque—rather like the
change in the white of an egg when it is boiled. An eye without
a lens will still form images but they are not focused on the
retina and appear blurred. Distinct vision may be restored by
spectacles, but since the eye no longer possesses the power of
accommodation, two pairs of spectacles, one for near, and one for
distant vision, are necessary.

Persistence of vision.

If a glowing splinter is moved rapidly it gives the appearance
momentarily of a continuous luminous line. This is due to the
fact that the sensation caused by an image on the retina lasts from

at least $\frac{1}{10}$th to $\frac{1}{8}$th of a second. Thus the splinter is seen in a large number of positions before the original sensation has faded. The phenomenon is known as the *persistence of vision*.

Again, the spokes of a rapidly revolving wheel cannot be distinguished. The sensations caused by the rapidly moving images on the retina are superimposed and hence hazy. If, however, only one image is permitted to be formed on the retina—by blinking, or, better still, by illuminating the wheel in a dark room with an electric spark (which lasts only 1/20,000th of a second)—a clear view of each spoke is obtained.

The production of continuous moving pictures in the cinema is only possible as a result of the persistence of vision. Twenty-four pictures (sixteen in some projectors), each slightly different from its predecessor, are thrown on to the screen each second, and give the appearance of continuity.

Binocular vision.

The advantage of having two eyes is that together they enable us to see things in relief. Each eye views its surroundings from a slightly different position and the images, therefore, on the retinas are not identical. The left eye sees more of the left side of an object than the right, and *vice versa*, enabling the solidity of an object to be appreciated.

The stereoscope is an instrument in which this fact is utilised. Two photographs of a landscape are taken from two slightly different view-points corresponding to the positions of a person's eyes. Each picture is presented to the appropriate eye with the result that the person sees the landscape in relief.

Again, the possession of two eyes enables distances to be judged. When both eyes are directed to an object the two eyeballs are slightly inclined so that their axes intersect at the object. From the muscular effort required to incline them, we obtain an estimate of the distance the object is away. This is not the only method we use for judging distances. The apparent diminished size of a distant object is a useful indication of its distance. Everyone knows how difficult it is to judge the distance of mountains seen across water, when there is no object of known size, such as a tree, to aid the judgment.

Since we have two eyes, why are not two images seen? The two images are formed on exactly corresponding parts of the retinas with the result that the sensations received by the brain are completely fused. If the images are not formed on corresponding parts of the retinas, two images are seen. Hold your two forefingers in a line with your nose, one about 10 in. away, and the other double this distance. Direct your eyes on the further finger. You will then see two images of the nearer finger. Remove the further finger and the two images will become clearer.

Defects of vision.

There are four main defects of vision:

1. *Short sight or myopia.*
2. *Long sight or hypermetropia.*
3. *Astigmatism.*
4. *Presbyopia.*

These defects may be overcome by using auxiliary lenses called spectacles. There is a legend that Nero wore an emerald monocle to correct his short sight. Roger Bacon (1214–94) suggested the idea of spectacles and they first came into use at the beginning of the fourteenth century. The latest type of spectacles, for those who feel that the wearing of spectacle frames detracts from their appearance, are contact glasses which fit on to the cornea. They consist of parallel-sided "dishes of glass" which fill with tears and hence effectively alter the curvature of the cornea to the appropriate extent. Although irksome at first, they are said to become comfortable after a time, like false teeth.

1. *Short sight.* A short-sighted professor cannot see the scholars at the back of his classroom (unless he is wearing spectacles). The defect is due to the eyeball being too long, so that even at its thinnest the crystalline lens has too short a focal length to focus distant objects on the retina (see Fig. 76a). The remedy is a diverging spectacle lens which causes the light to diverge before entering the eye and hence enables the image to be focused further back from the cornea (see Fig. 76b).

The nearest and furthest points which can be seen clearly and comfortably by a normal eye are called the *near point* and the *far point* respectively. The former is situated about 25 cm. or 10 in.

from the eye (*the least distance of distinct vision*) and the latter at infinity (see Fig. 77).

In the case of a short-sighted eye the far point is very much nearer than infinity. The near point also is nearer than normally: thus a short-sighted person, by raising spectacles on his forehead, can see finer detail on an object than a normal person because he can bring the object closer to his eye.

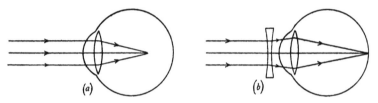

Fig. 76. (*a*) Short-sighted eye, (*b*) corrected by spectacle lens.

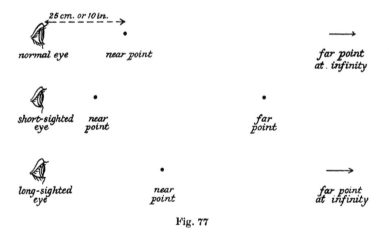

Fig. 77

Example. The furthest distance of distinct vision of a short-sighted person is 100 cm. What spectacles will he require in order to see distant objects clearly?

The function of the spectacle lens is to "bring up" an object from infinity to a distance of 200 cm. from the eye. The eye can then see it distinctly.

Applying the formula $\dfrac{1}{u} + \dfrac{1}{v} = \dfrac{1}{f}$ to the spectacle lens,

$$u = +\infty \text{ (infinity)},$$

$$v = -200 \text{ cm.},$$

$$\frac{1}{\infty} + \frac{1}{-200} = \frac{1}{f},$$

$$\frac{1}{-200} = \frac{1}{f}.$$

$$\therefore \ f = -200 \text{ cm.}$$

Hence diverging spectacles of 200 cm. focal length (or 0·5 dioptre power) are required.

2. *Long sight.* A long-sighted person can see distant objects very clearly but cannot see near objects distinctly. The defect is due to the eyeball being too short: the crystalline lens cannot

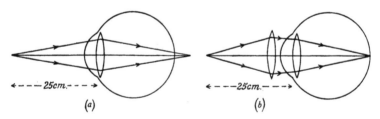

Fig. 78. (*a*) Long-sighted eye, (*b*) corrected by spectacle lens.

bulge sufficiently (without undue strain) to focus near objects on the retina (see Fig. 78*a*). A converging spectacle lens is necessary (see Fig. 78*b*).

Example. The near point of a long-sighted person is 50 cm. from the eye. What spectacles must he wear in order to read a book at a distance of 25 cm.?

The function of the spectacle lens is to "remove" an object at a distance of 25 cm. to a distance of 50 cm. from which it can be seen clearly by the eye.

Applying the formula $\dfrac{1}{u} + \dfrac{1}{v} = \dfrac{1}{f}$ to the spectacle lens,

$$u = +25 \text{ cm.,}$$
$$v = -50 \text{ cm.,}$$
$$\frac{1}{25} + \frac{1}{-50} = \frac{1}{f}.$$
$$\therefore f = 50 \text{ cm.}$$

Hence converging spectacles of 50 cm. focal length (or 2 dioptres power) are required.

3. *Astigmatism.* A person suffering from astigmatism on looking at Fig. 79 will see one line more sharply focused than the rest. This is due to the fact that his cornea is not accurately spherical but has a greater curvature in one direction than in others. The astigmatism is said to be regular when the lines of greatest and least curvature are at right angles. Such astigmatism can be corrected by using a cylindrical lens, either a positive one to aid the minimum curvature or a negative one to reduce the maximum curvature. Irregular astigmatism cannot as a rule be corrected. The term "astigmatism" is derived from the fact that an astigmatic eye cannot form a point image (*a*—not, *stigma*—a point).

Fig. 79

4. *Presbyopia.* Presbyopia is a loss of accommodating power, prevalent in elderly people whose ciliary muscles, in common with their other muscles, have become less supple. Two pairs of spectacles are required, or alternatively, a pair of bifocal lenses, the lower halves of which are used for reading and the upper halves for distant vision.

Eye testing.

The oculist tests eyes by means of a test-card containing lines of letters of different sizes. To be seen clearly by a normal eye the letters must subtend an angle of at least 5′ and the strokes of the letters 1'. Thus the line down to which one can read depends on the length of the oculist's consulting room.

Fig. 80 is a typical oculist's prescription. This prescription is for a person who is short-sighted and also suffers from astigmatism. Spherical diverging lenses with a power of 1 dioptre ($-1 \cdot 0$ D.sph.), in combination with cylindrical lenses of $-0 \cdot 75$ dioptre, are prescribed. The axes of the cylindrical lenses are denoted by an arrow marked with the angle 90°.

Two pairs of spectacles are printed on the prescription form, one for far and one for near vision, since persons suffering from presbyopia require two pairs, or one pair with bifocal lenses.

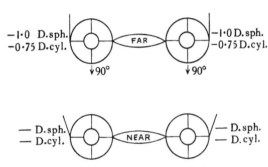

Fig. 80. An oculist's prescription.

SUMMARY

The photographic camera, the optical lantern, the epidiascope and the eye consist essentially of a converging lens which forms a real image.

The phenomenon of the persistence of vision is due to the fact that the sensation caused by an image on the retina takes an appreciable time to fade. Two eyes enable us to see objects in relief.

The eye suffers from the following defects:

1. Short sight—corrected by a diverging spectacle lens.
2. Long sight—corrected by a converging spectacle lens.
3. Astigmatism—corrected by a cylindrical spectacle lens.
4. Presbyopia.

QUESTIONS

1. What is the purpose of the stop in a photographic camera?

With a stop of $f/8$ the correct exposure is $\frac{1}{30}$ sec. What would be the exposure with a stop $f/32$?

2. Explain the optical system of a projecting lantern (the ordinary "magic" lantern). How would you decide what focal length of projecting lens to use in a given hall?   (O. & C.)

3. Explain, with a diagram, why lantern slides are put into a lantern upside down.

4. Compare the eye and the photographic camera pointing out their similarities and differences.

5. Draw a diagram of the eye, showing its structure, and state the purpose served by each of its chief parts.

Explain *two* of the following:

   (a) How the eye can focus near and far objects.

   (b) How the eye can adjust itself to lights of different intensity.

   (c) Why the spokes of a rapidly revolving wheel cannot be distinguished.   (O.)

6. What is meant by long sight and short sight and how may they be corrected?

A long-sighted person cannot see distinctly objects nearer than 50 cm. What kind of lens must he use in order that he may be able to read a book at distances down to 25 cm.?   (C.)

7. A short-sighted person can see distinctly objects which are not more than 12 in. from the eye. What kind of lens should he use, and of what focal length, to enable him to see clearly at 20 in.?   (O.)

8. Explain carefully:

   (a) The advantage of possessing two eyes. (Are these advantages shared by a hen?)

   (b) The power of a lens.

   (c) Astigmatism.

9. A short-sighted person cannot see distinctly objects which are less than 5 in., and more than 40 in., away. Calculate the focal length of the spectacles he requires in order to see distant objects distinctly. What will be his least distance of distinct vision when wearing these spectacles?

10. The least distance of distinct vision of a long-sighted person is reduced from 70 cm. to 25 cm. by spectacles. What is the power of the spectacles?

11. A person suffering from presbyopia (who has lost the power of accommodation) can see clearly only objects at a distance of 100 cm. What is the power of the spectacles required (a) for reading a book at a distance of 30 cm., (b) for viewing distant objects?

12. Explain fully why, on the cinema screen, the wheels of moving vehicles sometimes seem to be standing still and sometimes to be rotating backwards.

Chapter VI

SPHERICAL MIRRORS

Curved mirrors possess the property of forming real images. They can therefore be used instead of lenses—for example in telescopes.

Hold a lighted candle in front of and fairly near to a concave mirror, e.g. a curved shaving mirror, which is facing a distant wall. Move the candle backwards and forwards until a large inverted image of the candle flame is seen on the wall. Note that the image is only in focus when the candle is at a particular distance from the mirror.

If the candle is held very near to the mirror, no image can be thrown upon the wall. However, on looking into the mirror an erect and magnified image of the candle flame may be seen situated behind the mirror. In the same way a concave shaving mirror produces a magnified image of a chin held near to it.

Definitions.

The only curved mirrors which we shall consider in detail in this chapter are spherical mirrors, i.e. mirrors whose curvature is like part of the shell of a hollow sphere. These are of two types,

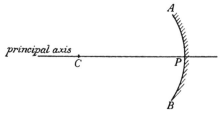

Fig. 81

concave and convex, according to whether the reflecting surface is the inside or outside of the spherical shell. Fig. 81 shows a concave mirror (*cavus*—a hollow). A shaving mirror is concave, whereas the driver's mirror at the side of a car is convex.

The middle point *P* of the surface of a spherical mirror is called *the pole* of the mirror, and the "width" *AB* of the mirror, its *aperture*. The centre of the sphere of which the mirror is part is called its *centre of curvature, C.* The length *PC* is the *radius of curvature,* and this line, produced if necessary, is called the *principal axis* of the mirror.

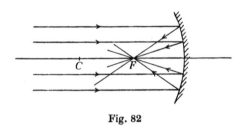

Fig. 82

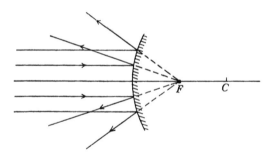

Fig. 83

The principal focus.

All rays parallel to the axis and incident on a concave mirror of small aperture are reflected through a point half way between the mirror and the centre of curvature, called the *principal focus,* *F* (see Fig. 82). We shall explain later why this is so. The distance *PF* is called the *focal length* of the mirror. Since the rays of light are reversible, if a point object is placed at *F*, rays from it, after reflection at the mirror, are rendered parallel to the axis

In the case of a convex mirror the principal focus, *F* (see Fig. 83), is virtual.

Graphical construction of the image.

In order to fix the position of the image formed by a spherical mirror it is necessary to trace only two rays from the top of the object. The point where the two reflected rays intersect will be the corresponding point of the image.

There are two convenient rays which can be drawn. They are:

1. *A ray parallel to the axis which is reflected through the principal focus, F.*

2. *A ray through the centre of curvature, C, which falls upon the mirror normally and is reflected back along its own path.*

(A third ray, incident through *F* and reflected parallel to the axis, is sometimes useful.)

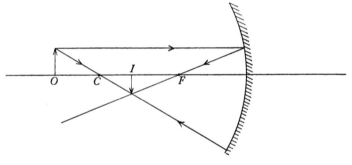

Fig. 84

These rays are drawn in Fig. 84. The image is drawn from their point of intersection, perpendicular to the axis. It will be seen that the image is real, inverted and diminished. The image is said to be real since the rays of light actually pass through it, with the result that it can be thrown upon a screen placed in the correct position to receive it. This is in contrast to a *virtual* image, such as is produced by a plane mirror. Rays of light do not pass through a virtual image; they only appear to come from it. Thus a virtual image cannot be thrown upon a screen.

The above graphical method enables the nature, size and position of the image to be determined accurately.

PLATE V

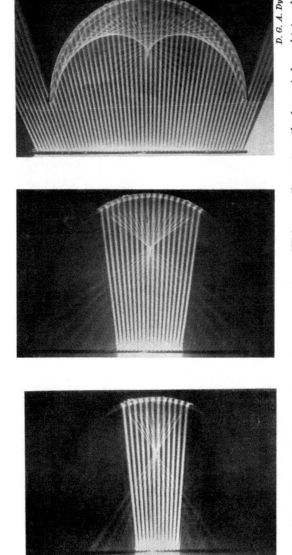

D. G. A. Dyson

The effect of increasing the aperture of a concave mirror. With a small aperture the beam is brought to what is practically a point focus. With a large aperture the reflected rays envelope a caustic, and a point image is not formed. The phenomenon is known as spherical aberration (see p. 102).

PLATE VI

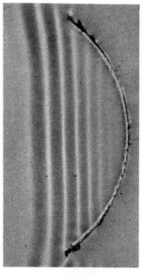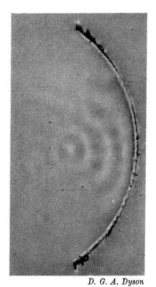

D. G. A. Dyson

(a)   (b)

Reflection of straight water waves at a concave mirror. After reflection the waves converge to the principal focus of the mirror.

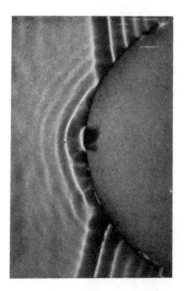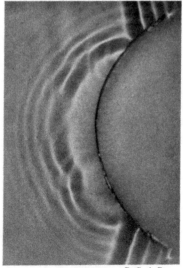

D. G. A. Dyson

(c)   (d)

Reflection of straight water waves at a convex mirror. After reflection the waves are curved and appear to be spreading from the principal focus behind the mirror.

Images formed by a concave mirror.

A man who is standing a great distance away from a large, vertical, concave mirror will see a small inverted image of himself. This image is situated very near to the principal focus, F, of the mirror.

As the man walks towards the mirror his image remains inverted but becomes gradually larger and moves from F towards C (see Fig. 84).

Image and man meet at C, and the image is now exactly the same size as the man, but still inverted (see Fig. 85). Note that in Fig. 85 a ray through the focus, which is reflected parallel to the axis, is drawn instead of the usual ray through C. (The man will not clearly see this

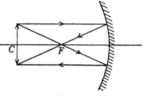

Fig. 85

image, however, nor the succeeding real images, since he cannot focus the light which forms them in his retina. The image begins to appear blurred as soon as it is nearer than the man's near point.)

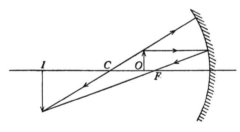

Fig. 86

As the man moves from C towards F the inverted image becomes magnified and moves beyond C with ever-increasing speed (see Fig. 86).

When the man reaches F his image is at infinity.

Now if the man walks just past F towards the mirror, his image appears suddenly clear on the other side of the mirror, a long way behind the silvering. It is virtual, erect, and magnified (see Fig. 87).

In Fig. 87 the rays behind the mirror are virtual rays. They do not actually exist and are therefore dotted. The rays which enter an eye in front of the mirror merely appear to be coming from the virtual image behind the mirror.

As the man walks still closer to the mirror, his image remains erect and virtual, but becomes less magnified and approaches him from behind the mirror.

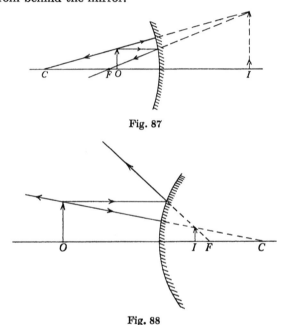

Fig. 87

Fig. 88

Images formed by a convex mirror.

The image formed by a convex mirror of a real object is always erect, virtual and diminished. In Fig. 88 two rays are traced from the top of the object O, a ray parallel to the axis reflected as though coming from F and a ray falling on the mirror in the direction of C reflected back along its own path. The point of intersection of the two reflected rays (produced) gives the position of the top of the image I. Note that rays behind the mirror are dotted since they are virtual.

Calculation of the position and height of the image.

If the same sign convention is used as for lenses (see p. 62) the same formula

$$\frac{1}{u} + \frac{1}{v} = \frac{1}{f} = \frac{2}{r}$$

may be used to calculate the position of all images formed by both concave and convex mirrors.

According to the convention **the radius of curvature and focal length of a concave mirror are positive: the radius of curvature and focal length of a convex mirror are negative.**

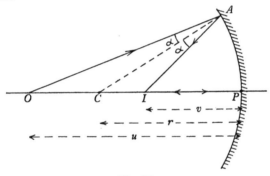

Fig. 89

The formula

$$\textbf{Magnification} = \frac{v}{u}$$

holds also for spherical mirrors as well as for lenses.

Proof of the formula $\quad \dfrac{1}{u} + \dfrac{1}{v} = \dfrac{2}{r}.$

When a ray of light is reflected at a curved mirror it obeys the laws of reflection which hold for reflection at a plane mirror. We can, therefore, assuming these laws of reflection, trace rays from an object and find the position of the image.

We will take the simplest possible case, a point object O (see Fig. 89) situated on the axis of the mirror. A ray from O along the axis strikes the mirror normally and returns along its own path. A ray OA is reflected along AI and cuts the reflected ray PO at I. We shall prove that all other reflected rays pass through I (so long as the aperture of the mirror is small), thus showing that I is the image of O.

We shall prove also the formula

$$\frac{1}{u}+\frac{1}{v}=\frac{2}{r},$$

where $u=$ distance of object from mirror PO, $v=$ distance of image from mirror PI, $r=$ radius of curvature of mirror PC.

This expression holds only if the aperture of the mirror is small: in Fig. 89 AP must be small.

Now the normal at A is the radius CA, C being the centre of curvature of the mirror. Since the second law of reflection holds

$$O\hat{A}C=C\hat{A}I.$$

Thus in $\triangle\ AIO$, AC is the bisector of $\hat{A}$.

$$\therefore \frac{AI}{AO}=\frac{IC}{CO} \quad \text{(theorem).}$$

If AP is small
$$AI=PI \text{ approx.,}$$
$$AO=PO \text{ approx.}$$
$$\therefore \frac{PI}{PO}=\frac{IC}{CO},$$
$$\text{i.e.} \quad \frac{v}{u}=\frac{r-v}{u-r},$$
$$ur-uv=uv-vr,$$
$$vr+ur=2uv.$$

Dividing through by uvr

$$\frac{1}{u}+\frac{1}{v}=\frac{2}{r}.$$

Whatever incident ray is drawn from O, so long as the point of incidence is near to P, the same expression will be obtained, and hence the same value for v. Thus all reflected rays must pass through I, and I is therefore the image of O.

Line object.

If the axis is revolved through a small angle about C (see Fig. 90) the object will trace out the path OO', and the image, the path II'. It is clear that our proof of the expression $\frac{1}{u}+\frac{1}{v}=\frac{2}{r}$ still holds if CP' is taken as the principal axis of the mirror instead of CP, since both CP and CP' are radii.

I' is therefore the image of O': similarly every point on II' is an image of a corresponding point on OO'. So long as PP' is small we can assume that OO' and II' are straight lines perpendicular to OCP. The expression $\dfrac{1}{u}+\dfrac{1}{v}=\dfrac{2}{r}$, therefore, holds for line objects at right angles to the axis as well as for point objects on the axis.

Proof that $f=\dfrac{r}{2}$.

We can prove that the focal length, f, is equal to half the radius of curvature from our formula. For if a point object is placed at F, the reflected rays, being parallel, will never meet, or, as the mathematicians say, they meet at infinity. Hence the image will be formed at infinity.

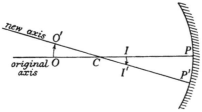

Fig. 90

Thus in the formula

$$\frac{1}{u}+\frac{1}{v}=\frac{2}{r},$$

$$u=f, \qquad v=\infty \quad \text{(infinity).}$$

$$\therefore \ \frac{1}{f}+\frac{1}{\infty}=\frac{2}{r}.$$

But $\dfrac{1}{\infty}=0 \left[\dfrac{1}{\text{million}} \text{ is small, } \dfrac{1}{\text{billion}} \text{ is smaller, and } \dfrac{1}{\text{infinity}} \text{ is } 0 \right]$.

$$\therefore \ \frac{1}{f}=\frac{2}{r},$$

$$f=\frac{r}{2}.$$

Our formula may therefore be written:

$$\frac{1}{u}+\frac{1}{v}=\frac{1}{f}.$$

Proof of the formula   *Magnification $=\dfrac{v}{u}$.*

In Fig. 91 a ray from the top of the object, OO', after reflection at the pole of the mirror, P, must pass through the top of the image II'. The angle of incidence is equal to the angle of reflection, i.e.

$$O'\hat{P}O = I\hat{P}I'.$$

Thus the right-angled triangles IPI' and OPO' are similar.

$$\therefore \quad \frac{II'}{OO'} = \frac{PI}{PO} = \frac{v}{u},$$

i.e. $\quad \dfrac{\text{height of image}}{\text{height of object}} = \dfrac{v}{u}.$

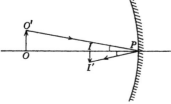

Fig. 91

Spherical aberration.

It was mentioned on p. 100 that the formula $\dfrac{1}{u} + \dfrac{1}{v} = \dfrac{2}{r}$ only holds for a mirror of small aperture. The fact is that a beam of light parallel to the principal axis of a concave mirror of large aperture is not reflected through a point focus but the reflected rays envelope a curve called a caustic, the cusp of which—the point of intersection of the two halves of the caustic—is at the principal focus (see Plate V, facing p. 96).

It is clear that if all reflected rays from a point on an object do not intersect in a point the image will be indistinct and distorted. This defect of the image is called spherical aberration.

A parabolic mirror brings a parallel beam of light to a point focus. Hence the reflector of a searchlight or the headlight of a car is a parabolic and not a spherical mirror. When a "point" source of light is placed at its focus all the rays are reflected in a comparatively parallel beam.

The reflection of waves at spherical mirrors.

On the corpuscular theory of light, reflection at spherical mirrors calls for no special explanation. The corpuscles bouncing, as it were, on the mirrors, follow the paths of the rays.

The reflection of waves at concave and convex mirrors is shown in Plate VI, facing p. 97.

EXPERIMENTS WITH SPHERICAL MIRRORS

EXPERIMENT 1. *To verify the formulae*

$$(a)\ \frac{1}{u}+\frac{1}{v}=\frac{2}{r} \qquad and \qquad (b)\ Magnification=\frac{v}{u}$$

for a concave mirror.

Using the apparatus described in Experiment 1, p. 68 (read the account of that experiment), focus an image of a luminous object on a screen by means of the concave mirror. Measure u, v, height of object and height of image. Repeat the experiment for different values of u and draw up a table.

EXPERIMENT 2. *Determination of the radius of curvature of a concave mirror.*

(a) The quickest method of making a rough determination of the radius of curvature of a concave mirror is to focus an image of a distant window on to a sheet of paper by means of the mirror. The distance between the mirror and the paper is approximately equal to the focal length $\left(\dfrac{r}{2}\right)$ of the mirror, since the object may be considered to be at infinity.

(b) Another method is to utilise the fact that an object placed at the centre of curvature of the mirror forms an image in the same position as the object (see Fig. 85).

Adjust the position of a luminous object so that the image is focused alongside the object. Then the distance from the cross wires to the centre of the mirror is equal to r.

(c) A more accurate method of carrying out the experiment is to use a pin or triangular paper flag instead of a luminous object, and to fix its position by the parallax method instead of focusing. (See the experimental details given in Experiment 2 (b), p. 71.)

(d) Another method is to obtain a series of pairs of values of u and v by placing a vertical pin in front of the mirror to serve as object and adjusting the position of another pin until there is no parallax between it and the image of the first pin. Calculate r by means of the formula

$$\frac{1}{u}+\frac{1}{v}=\frac{2}{r}.$$

EXPERIMENT 3. *Determination of the refractive index of a liquid.*

Lay a concave mirror on a horizontal table. Adjust a horizontal pin vertically above the mirror so that there is no parallax between itself and its image. The pin is then at the centre of curvature of the mirror, C. Measure CP (see Fig. 92).

Pour a little of the liquid into the mirror. The pin will now require to be lowered to a point O in order to coincide in position with its own image. Measure OP. It can be proved that

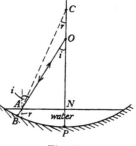

Refractive index of the liquid, $\mu = \dfrac{CP}{OP}$.

In Fig. 92 the ray OA, after refraction at the surface of the liquid, must proceed in the direction CAB, in order to strike the mirror normally and return along its own path.

Fig. 92

$$\therefore \mu = \frac{\sin i}{\sin r} = \frac{AN/NO}{AN/NC} = \frac{AC}{AO} = \frac{CP}{OP} \quad \text{(approx.)}.$$

Experiment 4. *Determination of the radius of curvature of a convex mirror.*

The image formed in a convex mirror is always virtual and behind the mirror, and hence its position is not easy to locate.

(*a*) Place a pin in front of a convex mirror. Place another pin behind the mirror with its upper part visible above the mirror, and adjust its position so that there is no parallax between it and the image of the first pin. Measure u and v, hence calculate r.

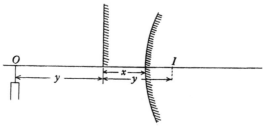

Fig. 93

This method is not very accurate, owing to the gap between the image and the second pin or distortion of the image near the periphery of the mirror.

(b) A better method is to place a plane mirror at right angles to the axis of the convex mirror so that it covers half the convex mirror (see Fig. 93). Move the plane mirror so that there is no parallax between the images formed in the two mirrors. Since the image formed by a plane mirror is as far behind the mirror as the object is in front, the position of the two images is known. Measure x and y. Then $v = -(y-x)$, $u = x+y$. Hence calculate r.

Summary

There are two types of spherical mirrors, concave and convex. The position and size of the image formed by a spherical mirror of small aperture may be calculated by means of the formulae

$$\frac{1}{u} + \frac{1}{v} = \frac{1}{f} = \frac{2}{r},$$

$$\text{Magnification} = \frac{\text{Height of image}}{\text{Height of object}} = \frac{v}{u},$$

where u = distance from the object to the mirror, v = distance from the mirror to the image, r = distance from the mirror to the centre of curvature (i.e. radius of curvature).

Distances actually travelled by the light are taken as positive, and distances along a virtual ray as negative. For a concave mirror r and f are positive; for a convex mirror they are negative.

Experimental determination of the radius of curvature.

1. *Concave mirror.*

(a) Rough focusing method using a distant window as object. Image is at principal focus.

(b) Determination of u and v using luminous object and focusing method. Then

$$\frac{1}{u} + \frac{1}{v} = \frac{2}{r}.$$

(c) Determination of u and v by pin-parallax method.

(d) Object at centre of curvature forms an image in same plane. Use focusing or pin-parallax method.

2. *Convex mirror.*

The determination of the radius of curvature of a convex mirror is difficult because the image is virtual and is formed behind the mirror.

(*a*) Rough pin-parallax method using a pin viewed over the top of mirror to locate the image.

(*b*) Pin-parallax method using a plane mirror.

QUESTIONS

1. Find by calculation and also by accurate drawing the position, height and nature of the image formed by a concave mirror of radius of curvature 10 cm. when an object of height 1·5 cm. is placed (*a*) 15 cm., (*b*) 3 cm. from it.

2. Find by calculation and also by accurate drawing the position, height and nature of the image formed by a convex mirror of radius of curvature 8 cm. when an object 2 cm. high is placed 6 cm. from it.

3. A man walks from a distance towards a large spherical concave mirror, some feet in diameter, which is mounted on a wall opposite to him. With the aid of a series of diagrams, show and explain the changes in the appearance of the image of himself which he sees.

4. State fully for what positions of the object a concave mirror forms (*a*) real, (*b*) virtual, (*c*) magnified, (*d*) diminished, (*e*) erect, (*f*) inverted images.

5. Describe a method of measuring the focal length of a concave mirror. The image of an object placed in front of a concave mirror is one-half the size of the object, and is 45 cm. from the object. What is the focal length of the mirror? (C.)

6. Distinguish between real and virtual images giving diagrams to illustrate their formation.

A real image is formed 40 cm. from a spherical mirror, the image being twice the size of the object. What kind of mirror is it, and what is the radius of curvature? (C.)

7. Define *radius of curvature* and *focal length of a concave mirror*. Prove that the radius of curvature is twice the focal length. A concave mirror of focal length 12 in. forms an upright image three times the size of the object. Determine the position of the object.

8. How would you employ a concave spherical reflector and a point source of light in order to make (*a*) a parallel beam, (*b*) a divergent beam of light?

If the radius of curvature of the mirror was 2 ft., and the light was placed 1 ft. 4 in. away from it, to what point would the beam converge after reflection? (N.)

9. Explain how a concave mirror is used to obtain a magnified, erect image of an object. Draw the pencil of rays by which a person would see a point on his chin by means of a concave mirror of 12 in. radius of curvature held 3 in. in front of his face. (Put the object point 2 in. below the axis and the eye 3 in. above and make the diagram half-size.)

10. A dentist holds a concave mirror of focal length 4·0 cm. at a distance of 1·5 cm. from a tooth. Find the position and magnification of the image which will be formed.

11. Assuming that the diameter of the moon is 2000 miles, and its distance from the earth 240,000 miles, find the diameter of the image of the moon produced by a concave mirror of radius 100 ft. (C.)

12. A concave mirror forms an image of a small object which is exactly the same size as the object when the latter is at a distance of 24 cm. from the mirror. Where must the object be placed for the mirror to form a real image of it which is 3·6 times the size of the object? Give diagrams to illustrate, in each case, how the image is formed. (C.)

13. A clearly lighted body stands upon the axis of a convex mirror, focal length 3 in., at a distance of 10 in. from the surface. Work out the details of magnification, position, and nature of the image that this information allows, and draw a diagram to illustrate your answer. (N.)

14. Define the principal focus of a convex spherical mirror, and state where it is situated.

A convex mirror has a radius of curvature of 6 in.; an object 2 in. long stands 2 in. in front of the mirror. Calculate the position and size of the image. Draw to scale a diagram showing the beam by which an eye, situated off the axis, sees one end of the object reflected in the mirror. (C.)

15. Prove the formula $\dfrac{1}{v} + \dfrac{1}{u} = \dfrac{2}{r}$ for reflection at a concave mirror.

How could you determine whether a mirror is plane, concave, or convex, without touching its surface? (L.)

16. Explain why the reflecting mirrors of motor-cars are usually convex.

17. Draw a diagram to show why a concave mirror gives a sharper image if only the central portion of the mirror is used.

18. Small electric torches are usually made with a concave reflector behind the filament and a convex lens in front of it. Show how either of these separately could produce a parallel beam of light, and indicate the best position in which these could be used in conjunction for this purpose.   (N.)

19. A pin is set up 30 cm. in front of a convex mirror. It is found that if a plane mirror is placed between the pin and the convex mirror 20 cm. from the pin (so that it covers only half the convex mirror) the images of the pin in both convex and plane mirrors coincide. Find the radius of curvature of the convex mirror.

20. A pin placed 20 cm. above a concave mirror lying on a bench is found to coincide in position with its own image. When a little turpentine is poured into the mirror, the pin must be lowered through a distance of 6·4 cm. before there is again no parallax between it and its image. Find the refractive index of turpentine.

Chapter VII

DISPERSION

It was known to the ancients that when white light is passed through glass of certain shapes it emerges as light of many colours. Colourless glass produces this effect, and there is no question therefore of colour in the glass producing colours in the light.

The phenomenon, known as dispersion, was investigated by Sir Isaac Newton. "In the year 1666 (at which time I applied myself to the grinding of optick glasses other than spherical) I procured me a triangular glass prism to try therewith the celebrated phenomena of colours." He darkened his room in

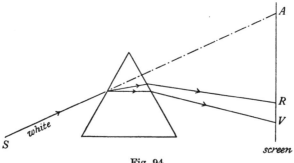

Fig. 94

Trinity College, Cambridge, and in the shutters made a small circular hole, about ⅓ in. in diameter, through which sunlight streamed forming a white circular patch on the opposite wall. He then interposed his glass prism in the path of the beam. An elongated coloured patch of light, five times as long as it was broad and having semicircular ends of red and violet, was formed on the wall instead of the white circular patch. Newton called the coloured band a "spectrum". Its colours are those of the rainbow—violet, blue, green, yellow, orange, red—with the shade of each colour merging imperceptibly into the next.

It will be seen from Fig. 94 that besides being split up into colours, the light on passing through the prism is also much deviated. Note that, in order to represent Newton's arrangement, this figure would need to be turned upside down. It is usual, however, to draw a prism with its refracting edge uppermost.

Before Newton's time it was assumed that the prism inserted the colours into the white light. Barrow, Newton's tutor at Cambridge, held an obscure theory that the violet light is white light rarefied, and red light is white light condensed.

Newton tried several hypotheses to account for the phenomenon. He toyed, for instance, with the idea that rays of light might be made to describe a curved path in passing through the

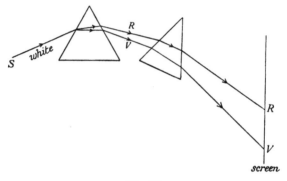

Fig. 95

prism, just as a tennis ball may be made to describe a curved path by giving it "spin" with a racket. Different rays, he thought, might be curved to a different extent, and so produce different colours. He thought of light on the corpuscular theory as consisting of a stream of corpuscles, like tiny balls. But he could detect no such curvature in the emergent rays.

Eventually he came to the conclusion that **a beam of white light is simply a bundle of different coloured rays, and that the glass prism sorts them out because glass has a different refractive index for light of different colours.** The refractive index is smallest for red light, and therefore on passing through the prism the red light is bent the least; the refractive index for violet light is the greatest, and therefore the violet light is bent the most; and the other colours, being bent to an intermediate extent, form a coloured band between.

Newton supported his theory by a series of simple but conclusive experiments.

Newton's experiments in support of his theory.

1. *A second prism gives no further colour.* Pass light through two prisms as in Fig. 95. The spectrum *RV* is elongated but no further colours are added by the second prism. The first prism has sorted out the colours in the white light and the second prism merely deviates each colour further.

2. *A second reversed prism recombines the colours to form white light.* Pass white light through reversed prisms as in Fig. 96. When the screen is placed at a certain distance away a white

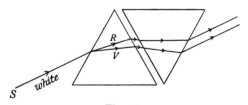

Fig. 96

patch is formed upon it. The first prism sorts out the colours, and the second prism recombines them. In Fig. 96 only one incident ray is drawn and it gives rise to an emergent beam of parallel coloured rays. In practice there are always a large number of parallel incident rays and the emergent beams overlap giving a resultant white emergent beam, coloured imperceptibly at its edges.

3. *Light of a single colour is merely deviated by a second prism. No fresh colour is added.* Allow light of one colour, say the red, formed from white light by a prism, to pass through a slit in a screen, and fall upon a second prism as in Fig. 97. The second prism merely deviates the red ray, and does not change its colour: moreover, it deviates the violet ray (when that is allowed to fall upon it) more than it does the red.

Although these experiments are now regarded as conclusive proof of Newton's theory, they were not universally accepted by his contemporaries. Newton, always extraordinarily sensitive to criticism, wrote to Leibnitz, "I was so persecuted with discussions arising from the publication of my theory of light, that I blamed my own imprudence for parting with so substantial a blessing as my quiet, to run after a shadow".

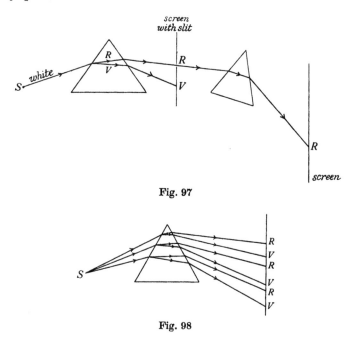

Fig. 97

Fig. 98

Production of a pure spectrum.

When light from a small source is passed through a prism (see Fig. 98) considerable overlapping of the colours occurs in the resulting spectrum. This impure spectrum will be red at one end, violet at the other, but a yellowish white in the middle where the colours have recombined.

In Newton's experiment the rays of sunlight falling on his prism were practically parallel since the source from which they came was 93 million miles away. Hence rays of each colour issued from the prism as a parallel beam, and formed on the wall a circular coloured patch, because the hole in the screen was circular. Six of these coloured patches have been drawn in Fig. 99. According to Newton's own measurements, they have to be fitted into a spectrum five times as long as each patch. Hence considerable overlapping must have taken place, and Newton's spectrum was by no means pure.

Again, Newton picked out what he considered to be the most prominent colours in the spectrum, violet, blue, green, yellow, orange, red (VBGYOR). (Newton included indigo, between the violet and the blue, but most people cannot distinguish it.) But there are really an infinite number of colours in the spectrum. It is no more

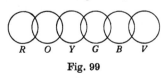

R   O   Y   G   B   V

Fig. 99

possible to say how many colours there are than it is possible to say how many points there are in a line of certain length. Moreover, we have only a limited number of names for colours and the word "red", for example, has to cover a wide range of tints. Thus Newton's spectrum was the result of innumerable overlapping images of different colours, and far more impure than is represented in Fig. 99.

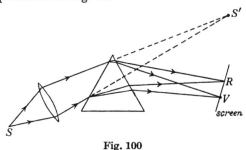

Fig. 100

To obtain a pure spectrum it is necessary to have as a source a brightly illuminated slit, as narrow as possible. Form a distant image of this slit on a screen by means of a convergent lens. Now interpose the prism in the path of the light (see Fig. 100). Since the light will be deviated, the screen must be moved, but, in order to keep the image in focus, the screen must be kept at the same distance from the prism. An infinite series of coloured images of the slit will be focused side by side on the screen, forming a pure spectrum.

If the prism is turned the spectrum will be seen to move and alter in length. When the prism is in the minimum deviation position, the spectrum is shortest, brightest and clearest.

Explanation of dispersion.

Newton's experiments established the fact that white light is not homogeneous but consists of light of many colours, all of which are refracted to a different extent by a medium such as glass.

Now the refraction of light as it passes from air into glass is caused by a reduction of velocity (see p. 35). While lights of all colours travel with the same velocity in air their velocities differ when they enter glass, red light being the least retarded and violet the most. Hence red light suffers the least refraction and violet the most.

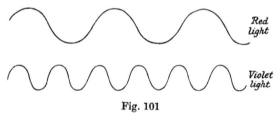

Fig. 101

According to the wave theory the red waves travel faster in glass than the violet waves owing to the fact that they have the longer wave-length (see Fig. 101).

We will illustrate the argument by means of an analogy. Suppose a number of men and a number of boys are walking together along a road. The boys have a shorter stride but by making more strides to the minute they can keep pace with the men. If, however, their route changes from a road to a ploughed field, the roughness of the ground will impede the progress of both men and boys at each stride they take. Owing to the fact that they take more strides than the men per minute, the boys will be the more impeded. If the amount of energy expended by both men and boys remains constant, the pace of both will be retarded, but the boys will gradually be left behind.

Recombining the colours of the spectrum to form white light.

(a) *Using a colour disc.* We have described, in the earlier part of this chapter, only those experiments in support of his theory which Newton devised with prisms. But there are two other convincing experiments, also due to Newton, which show that when all the colours of the spectrum enter the eye simultaneously the sensation of white is experienced.

Paint the colours of the spectrum in suitable proportions on a cardboard disc in sectors, and revolve the disc at speed, preferably by an electric motor. The coloured disc looks white.

Owing to what is called the persistence of vision, the eye cannot get rid of the sensation of an image on the retina in less than a small fraction of a second. It is on this principle that the cinematograph works. Images are thrown on to the screen at the rate of 16 or 24 per second, and give the impression of continuity. Thus in the colour disc experiment the various colours of the spectrum are superimposed on the retina and act upon it simultaneously, giving the sensation of white.

It should be added that owing to the difficulty of painting colours in the correct tint and proportion, perfect results are not easily attainable with a home-made disc. Specially prepared ones are generally more satisfactory. They should be strongly illuminated.

This experiment also lends itself to determining what colour sensation the brain will receive when lights of different colours and in different proportions enter the eye simultaneously, a problem which we shall consider in the next chapter.

Discs of different colours, cut along a radius so that they can be fitted together leaving portions of each exposed, may be revolved together.

(b) *Using a lens.* The light of different colours forming a spectrum can be recombined to form white light by means of a lens.

Form a spectrum by means of a glass prism, in the usual way, a short distance in front of a converging lens of about 10 cm. focal length (see Fig. 102). Move the lens until the point marked *O* in the figure is focused on the screen at *I*. This can be done (roughly) by placing a stop against the prism and focusing the image of its edge on the screen. The beam *RV* (whose colours

may be demonstrated by placing a piece of paper in it) gives rise
to a white patch at I.

This arrangement can also be used to determine what effect
on the resulting colour of the light is caused by extracting
certain colours from the spectrum. Thus if the red is eliminated
by placing a thin opaque strip in the way of the red light the
colour of the image on the screen is a greeny blue called peacock
blue. Two colours, such as red and peacock blue, which together
form white, are said to be *complementary colours*.

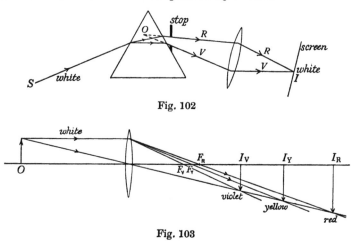

Fig. 102

Fig. 103

Similarly, slits can be arranged in the plane of the spectrum
(in front of the lens), and only light of certain colours allowed
through. Sir William Abney elaborated this method for the
study of colour vision.

Chromatic aberration.

Since glass has a smaller refractive index for red than for violet
light the focal length of a lens is greater for red light than for
violet light. In Fig. 103, I_V, I_Y, I_R are the images formed by a
converging lens of an object O in violet, yellow and red light,
F_V, F_Y, F_R being the foci for light of these colours. The positions
of the images may be determined experimentally by using a
luminous object in front of which is placed a violet, yellow or red

filter and by focusing the images on a screen. White light is dispersed by the lens and it is evident from Fig. 103 that, if a screen is placed at I_Y, the image of a white object (using no filter) will have a coloured fringe at its edge. This defect of the image is known as *chromatic aberration*.

Newton came to the conclusion that the defect was ineradicable, since it was inherent in the nature of light itself. It followed that large, efficient, refracting telescopes were impracticable, and he therefore concentrated his attention on reflectors.

We know now, however, that chromatic aberration can be cured. Let us first consider the case of prisms.

We must at the outset distinguish carefully between deviation and dispersion (see Fig. 104). The *deviation* produced by a prism is the angle between the *incident and emergent rays* when light of

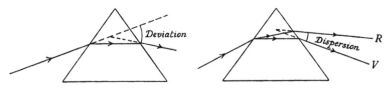

Fig. 104

a particular colour—say yellow sodium light—is refracted. The *dispersion* produced by a prism is the angle between the *emergent red and violet rays* when a beam of white light is refracted. Thus the spectrum produced by a hollow prism containing water is much shorter than that produced by a glass prism of the same angle: the dispersion is smaller.

Newton believed, erroneously, that deviation and dispersion were proportional for all materials, so that deviation is impossible without dispersion. In Fig. 96, by using a second reversed prism, dispersion has been eliminated, but there is no deviation: the final emergent beam is parallel to the incident beam.

Now flint glass has a dispersive power about twice that of crown glass, and hence a flint glass prism with half the angle of a crown glass prism will give equal (and opposite, if suitably placed) dispersion. Its refractive index is not twice as great, however, and therefore the deviation is not all annulled. Two such prisms are called an achromatic combination. It will be seen from Fig. 105 that a single ray of white light gives rise to a narrow emergent beam of parallel coloured rays: in practice the emergent beam is white and coloured imperceptibly at its edges since the emergent beams caused by a number of incident rays overlap.

Similarly, a converging achromatic combination of lenses may be made (see Fig. 106). A converging lens of crown glass is combined with a diverging lens of flint glass, the latter having

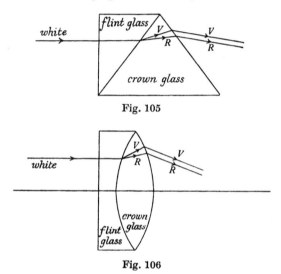

Fig. 105

Fig. 106

half the power, i.e. twice the focal length. The combination will be converging. The lenses may be regarded for any particular ray as two reversed prisms.

High-powered microscopes and refracting telescopes would have been an impossibility had not the secret of achromatic combinations been discovered.

The rainbow.

The rainbow is caused by the dispersion of sunlight in raindrops in the air.

When white light enters a spherical water drop the violet rays are more refracted than the red. Consequently, after one internal reflection, the violet rays emerge more deviated than the red (see Fig. 107). If the eye is placed in such a position that these rays enter it, a spectrum will be seen red on its upper side, and violet on its lower side, since, although the red rays emerge below the violet rays, they make a larger angle with the horizontal than the violet.

But besides the colours of the rainbow we have also to explain why it has the shape of a bow. Descartes gave the correct explanation in 1637, using Snell's law of refraction which had been discovered some years earlier. He drew the paths of the refracted

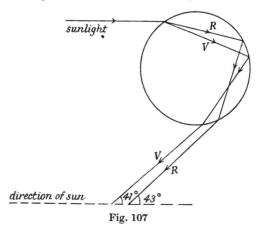

Fig. 107

and emergent rays of 10,000 parallel rays incident on one side of a drop. He found that the emergent rays issued in all directions, but that about 100 of these rays were all packed into a narrow, comparatively parallel, beam. These rays had suffered approximately minimum deviation. He came to the conclusion that only this narrow tightly packed beam was sufficiently intense to affect the eye. Hence only those drops which are in a position to send this beam to the eye take part in forming the rainbow. Since they must all subtend the same angle at the eye, they must lie on the surface of a cone with its apex at the eye. Hence the rainbow appears to have the shape of a bow. In Fig. 108 only a few raindrops at the top of the cone are shown. It is clear that if a number of men stand in a line they will all see a different rainbow, for a different set of raindrops will lie in the appropriate direction for each man. Also, of course, as the drops are falling the ones responsible for each bow are continually changing.

Sometimes a secondary bow, with the colours reversed (i.e. red on the lower side and violet on the upper), and higher in the sky, is seen. This is formed by light which suffers two internal reflections in raindrops (see Fig. 109).

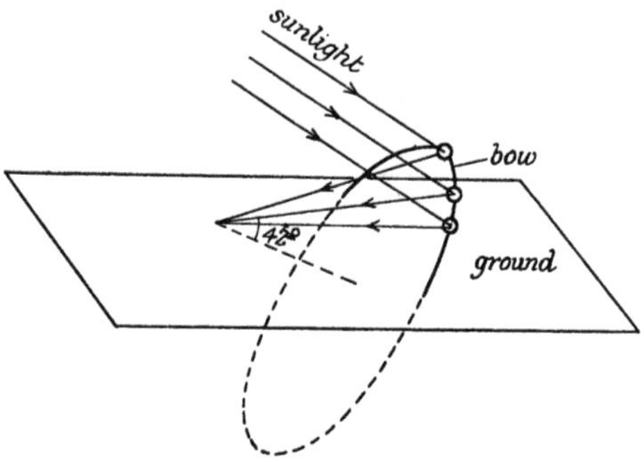

Fig. 108

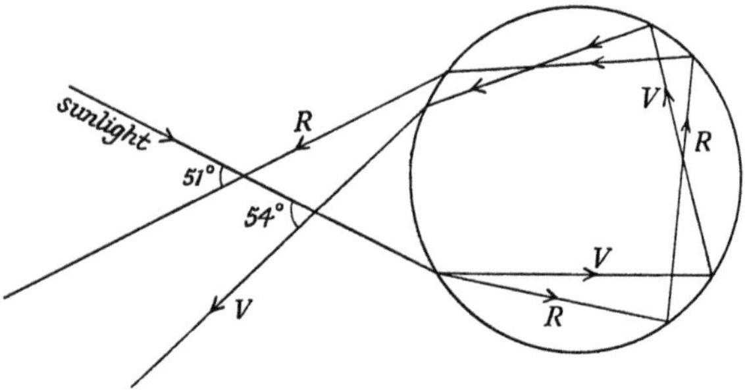

Fig. 109

Bows can also be seen wherever water breaks up into drops in sunlight, at the foot of a waterfall for example.

The spectrometer.

An instrument for producing and measuring pure spectra, called the spectrometer, is of the utmost importance to both the physicist and the astronomer. A picture of a spectrometer is shown in Fig. 110 and its optical arrangement is given in Fig. 111.

It consists of a tube called a collimator for producing a parallel beam of light and a telescope for viewing the light after it has emerged from a prism. The collimator consists of a vertical slit S (see Fig. 111), situated at the principal focus of a converging

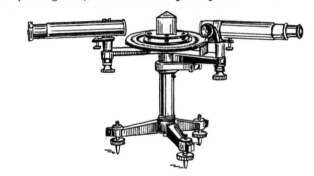

Fig. 110. Spectrometer.

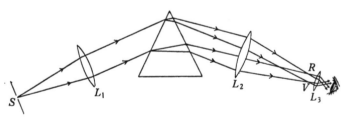

Fig. 111

lens L_1. When a source of light is placed in front of the slit, light from the slit falls upon L_1 and emerges as a parallel beam. The beam falls upon a prism, mounted on a small turn-table, and is dispersed. Each of the parallel beams of coloured light emerging from the prism is brought to a separate focus in the focal plane of the objective of the telescope, and forms a pure spectrum. The spectrum is viewed by the eyepiece of the telescope L_3 represented in Fig. 111 by a single lens, but in practice consisting of two lenses.

In the plane where the spectrum is formed there is a vertical cross-wire. The telescope can be turned about a circular scale, graduated in degrees, so that the vertical cross-wire falls on any part of the spectrum and hence the position of a point in the spectrum may be read.

It is of interest to compare the pure spectrum formed by the spectrometer with that formed by the arrangement shown in Fig. 100. The spectrometer arrangement is superior because, by rendering the beam of light parallel before it falls on the prism, every ray of light of a particular colour can be made to suffer minimum deviation (with the prism in the correct position) and in this position the coloured image of the slit is sharpest.

SPECTRA

The first advance in the study of spectra, after the time of Newton, occurred in the middle of the eighteenth century. It was known that the salts of certain metals, when placed in a flame, coloured it. Thus sodium gives a yellow flame, strontium a crimson flame, calcium a red flame, and potassium a lilac flame. The spectrum of each of these coloured flames was examined and it was found to consist, not of a whole continuous spectrum, nor even of a portion of a spectrum, but of a few brightly coloured lines, i.e. of a few separate coloured images of the slit. Sodium gives a yellow line, or more accurately, two yellow lines very close together. Strontium gives a number of red lines and a bright blue line. Calcium gives several red and yellow lines. Potassium gives two red lines and a violet line (see Frontispiece).

Now it must be borne in mind that an instrument like a spectrometer merely analyses the light which falls upon it. It enables us to examine the constituents of light. The light from any visible object is bound to give a spectrum, but the light from a non-luminous object, unless it is intensely illuminated, will be too dim to give a very bright spectrum.

We see, therefore, that the light from the coloured flames mentioned above consists of a few monochromatic colours. After considerable research it was shown that the bright spectral lines given by an element were characteristic of that element, and given by that element alone. The spectrometer was thus found to be a very delicate chemical detector for ascertaining the presence of certain elements. At first the fact that the yellow sodium line seemed always to be present in all spectra was a great source of confusion. But it was proved that as small a quantity of sodium as one thirty-thousand-millionth of a gram of sodium could be detected by a spectrometer and this amount of impurity may well be derived from the dust in the atmosphere.

The study of spectra was placed on a firm scientific basis by the researches in 1859 and 1860 of Bunsen and Kirchhoff. They discovered that the residue from a mineral water occurring naturally at Dürkheim gave two spectral lines, one a blue, and the other a red, which could not be attributed to any known element. They found that these lines are caused by two new elements which they called caesium (blue) and rubidium (red), after the colours of the lines. Several other elements were discovered in this manner, notably helium, which was found to exist in the sun before its presence on the earth was known.

Emission spectra.

There are two main types of spectra given by luminous bodies, known as emission spectra:

1. *Continuous spectra*—given by incandescent solids and liquids (e.g. the sun, white hot iron, molten silver, etc.).

2. *Bright line spectra*—given by incandescent vapours and gases (e.g. coloured flames or arcs, electric sparks, vacuum tubes).

Additional methods of producing bright line spectra.

A heavy element, such as iron, will not colour a bunsen flame. New methods were therefore devised for rendering such elements into the form of an incandescent vapour. We shall mention three methods:

1. The electric arc is the most intensely hot flame known. In it a metal such as iron may be vaporised. The spectrum of iron is found to consist of a large number of lines. A beautiful line spectrum is given by the mercury (arc) vapour lamp (see Frontispiece).

2. If an electric spark is passed between two metal electrodes and the light emitted by the spark analysed by a spectrometer, the resulting spectrum is found to be that of the metal of which the electrodes are composed. However, a number of lines due to the surrounding gas appear. Moreover, the spectrum changes

slightly when a greater quantity of electricity is passed. Great caution and discrimination must be exercised, therefore, when examining spectra since the same element under different conditions will give different lines.

3. If an electric discharge is passed through a rarefied gas (at a pressure of about 1 mm. of mercury) the gas becomes luminous, and the light emitted may be analysed by a spectrometer. A vacuum tube, as it is called, which is used for this purpose is shown in Fig. 112. The electric current is passed in and out by the metal electrodes at the ends. By constricting the tube in the middle a much brighter glow is obtained. (The red neon lamps used in advertisement signs are discharge tubes of the same type.)

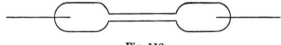

Fig. 112

A vacuum tube containing hydrogen gives a bright pink glow. The resulting spectrum consists of a number of lines (see Frontispiece). We shall have occasion to refer later to two of these lines, a bright red line called the C line and a bright blue line called the F line.

Absorption spectra.

In the year 1802 the English chemist Wollaston discovered that the spectrum of sunlight is crossed by seven dark lines. He suggested that the five most prominent of these lines were the boundaries of the most important colours in the spectrum. Cajori makes the following comment: "His explanation is of interest for it shows how a most plausible theory may be destitute of all truth."

In 1814 Fraunhofer, who was working in a glass works at Munich which manufactured telescope lenses, discovered that the spectrum of sunlight is crossed by hundreds of dark lines, and he mapped out 576 of them. His discovery was due to the fact that he was probably the first man to obtain a really pure spectrum. You should examine these lines for yourself. Shine sunlight on to the slit of an adjusted spectrometer.

The lines are called Fraunhofer lines. The most prominent of them were labelled with the letters A to K by their discoverer.

It was then found that these dark lines correspond in position to the bright lines of certain elements. The D line, for instance, corresponds to the (double) yellow sodium line, and the C and F lines to the red and blue lines of hydrogen.

The natural deduction was drawn that sunlight is deficient in the particular colours represented by the dark Fraunhofer lines. Foucault therefore tried to insert the colours by passing sunlight through an electric arc. He made the surprising discovery that so far from the dark lines disappearing they became more pronounced than before.

The true explanation of the lines was provided by Kirchhoff (although Stokes seems to have some claim to have found the explanation earlier). The sun consists of an intensely hot core called the photosphere, the surface of which is the part of the sun that we normally see, and a surrounding layer of cooler gases, called the reversing layer. Some of the light from the photosphere is absorbed as it passes through the cooler gases of the reversing layer.

We can, by a simple and beautiful experiment, demonstrate this process in the laboratory. Set up a sodium flame in front of the slit of a carefully adjusted spectrometer. Turn the telescope until the yellow sodium line is in view. Now pass light from a lantern containing a 500 candle-power lamp (or an electric arc) through the sodium flame on to the spectrometer slit. A continuous spectrum will be seen with the sodium line reversed, i.e. dark. It is essential that the source of white light should be at a higher temperature than the sodium flame.

A spectrum crossed by dark lines or bands is called an absorption spectrum. It is found that all substances absorb light of the same colour which they emit, provided that the source of the light is at a higher temperature than the substance in question.

Thus the Fraunhofer lines enable us to determine the composition of the reversing layer, i.e. the layer of comparatively cool gases round the photosphere. Helmholtz wrote of Kirchhoff's explanation of the Fraunhofer lines: " It has excited the admiration and stimulated the fancy of men as hardly any other discovery has done because it has permitted an insight into worlds that seemed forever veiled to us." To-day, the study of the spectra of the stars, which are similar to the sun but with individual variations, is one of the most important branches of astronomy. The spectrometer has revealed to us that the whole universe is made up of much the same elements which go to make up our own solar system.

Absorption spectra may be classified in a manner similar to that used for emission spectra.

Absorption spectra.

1. *Continuous absorption spectra.* When a filter (a piece of coloured gelatine or glass) is placed in front of light forming a spectrum a whole portion of the spectrum is wiped out. A solution of blood gives dark bands in the orange and yellow and absorbs all the violet (see Frontispiece). This is an important blood test.

2. *Line absorption spectra.* E.g. spectrum of sunlight or intense white light passed through a sodium flame or other vapours of elements.

How atoms emit light. The Rutherford-Bohr atom.

The light forming the bright lines of the spectrum is emitted by the atoms (the ultimate particles of matter), and is invaluable evidence in the consideration of atomic structure.

An atom may be regarded as a kind of miniature solar system. There is a small but massive nucleus, corresponding to the sun, round which revolve tiny particles of negative electricity called electrons, corresponding to the planets. Hydrogen has one revolving electron, helium two, lithium three, and so on up to uranium with 92.

Unlike the planets the electrons can move round the nucleus in a number of orbits. When an atom is violently buffeted by its neighbours, in a flame for example, an electron may be knocked into an outer orbit, like a ball being thrown from a lower to an upper stair, each stair representing a possible orbit. The atom thereby gains energy. Soon the electron jumps back, like the ball falling back to a lower stair, and gives out light in the process. The colour of the light depends on the position of the two orbits concerned. Thus each bright line in the spectrum corresponds to an electron falling from one orbit to an inner orbit.

We have mentioned that the spectrum of an element varies somewhat according to its mode of excitation. Additional lines appear when the atoms are more intensely excited because the electrons are knocked further out of the atoms and there are more transitions which they must make in returning. Again, if one electron is completely lost, the remainder will give a different set of lines (spark lines).

We have seen that atoms absorb light of exactly the same colour that they emit (absorption spectra). When light is absorbed an electron jumps from an inner to an outer orbit: on the return jump light of the same colour is emitted.

The infra-red and the ultra-violet.

Sir William Herschel in the year 1800 placed the bulb of a thermometer in different parts of the solar spectrum. He made the surprising discovery that the heating effect continues on moving the thermometer for a considerable distance beyond the red. There is, therefore, a large portion of the solar spectrum which is invisible to the eye, but which, like the visible part, can be detected by its heating effect (and also by means of a specially prepared photographic plate). These radiations, of longer wave-length than the visible, are called the *infra-red*.

The year following Herschel's discovery of the infra-red, Ritter discovered, by its action in blackening certain silver salts, a band of invisible radiation beyond the violet, called the *ultra-violet*.

If a test-tube containing quinine sulphate solution is placed in the ultra-violet it glows with a bluish light. This phenomenon is known as fluorescence and is shown by many other substances such as vaseline, lubricating oil and uranium glass. The energy of the short invisible ultra-violet waves is absorbed by the quinine sulphate, and re-emitted as visible light of longer wave-length.

Ultra-violet rays affect a photographic plate and can therefore be photographed. They have a beneficial effect on the human body, accelerating the manufacture of vitamin D under the skin, and therefore used as a curative for debility or diseases caused by a deficiency of this vitamin, or of sunlight.

The complete aether spectrum.

Wireless waves travel with the same velocity as light. They are believed to consist, like light, of waves in the aether. The wave-length of the wireless waves sent out by the Droitwich National transmitter is 1500 metres, about 1 mile. However, wireless waves have been produced of wave-length as small as the longest infra-red rays. Transmission on these extremely short wireless waves would therefore be subject to interference from the ordinary domestic fire.

At the other end of the scale there are extraordinary minute aether waves called X-rays, and shorter still γ-rays, emitted by radioactive substances. Fig. 113 represents what we may call the complete aether spectrum.

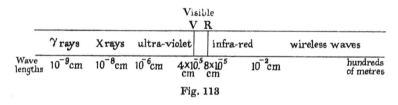

Fig. 113

SUMMARY

When white light passes through a prism (of glass for example) it is dispersed into the colours of the spectrum (VBGYOR). White light may be regarded as consisting of light of many colours for which a medium like glass has different refractive indices: $\mu_v > \mu_r$. The velocity of red light in glass is greater than the velocity of violet light.

A lens has a greater focal length for red light than for violet light. This causes coloration of the image, a defect known as chromatic aberration, which can be cured by using a compound lens of two kinds of glass, e.g. crown and flint glass.

The rainbow is caused by the dispersion of sunlight in raindrops in the air.

Spectra may be examined by an instrument called a spectrometer. They may be classified as follows:

1. *Emission spectra.*

    (*a*) Continuous (incandescent solids and liquids).

    (*b*) Bright line (incandescent vapours).

2. *Absorption spectra.*

    (*a*) Continuous (solids and liquids).

    (*b*) Line (vapours).

The invisible spectrum of sunlight consists of the ultra-violet and the infra-red.

PLATE VII

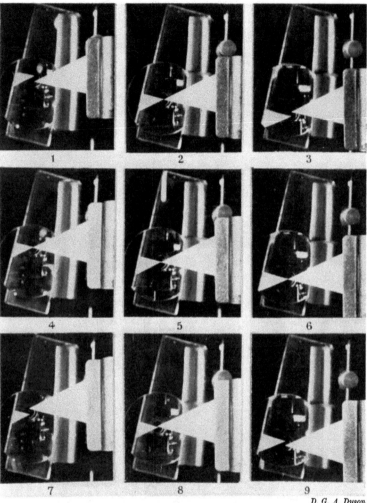

No-parallax adjustment in the determination of the focal length of a converging lens (see Fig. 67). The object, which is here horizontal, is the white paper flag on the right. It is not near enough to the lens in the top row, at the correct distance in the middle row, and too near the lens in the bottom row. Although the tips of the object and image coincide in 2 they move apart in 1 and 3 when the camera, which takes the place of the eye and whose reflection can be clearly seen, is moved up and down. In 4, 5 and 6 there is no parallax, and object and image stay together whatever the position of the camera. In 8 there is apparently a correct adjustment until, on moving the camera up and down (7 and 9), object and image move apart.

PLATE VIII

D. G. A. Dyson

Two photographs of the same scene, the upper one on an ordinary plate, and the lower one on an infra-red plate using an infra-red filter. Note how the details of the distant hills and the clouds are brought out in the infra-red picture. The picture was taken from near Stratford-on-Avon and the hill on the right, Bredon Hill, was 20 miles from the camera (see also p. 138).

QUESTIONS

1. Explain how a prism produces a spectrum and describe the arrangements you would make to project a pure spectrum on a screen.

2. Describe and explain the kind of spectra you would expect to observe from the following:

(a) a red-hot poker;

(b) a white-hot poker;

(c) the light from an electric lamp after passing through purple glass;

(d) a salt volatilised in a bunsen flame;

(e) the light of the sun.

3. How would you arrange an adjustable slit, two convex lenses, and a glass prism so as to produce a pure spectrum on a screen? What would be a suitable source of light for the experiment? What would be the effect produced in the appearance of the spectrum (a) if the slit were made wide, (b) if a sheet of red glass were interposed between the source of light and the rest of the apparatus? Give your reasons.

4. Describe the principal parts of a spectroscope and explain their action. What would be the nature of the spectra of the following sources of light: (a) an electric bulb, (b) the sun, (c) a neon lamp?

5. Explain fully why the bars of a window frame appear to be coloured when viewed through a glass prism.

6. The spectrum of the sun is a band of colours crossed by a number of dark lines. What is the explanation of this phenomenon? Would you expect the spectrum of moonlight to be crossed by dark lines also? Give your reasons.

7. (a) Explain the formation of colours in a rainbow.

(b) In what part of the sky is a rainbow seen in the early morning? Why is a rainbow never seen at mid-day except in winter?

(c) How would the appearance of a rainbow change to a man ascending vertically from the ground in a balloon?

8. Light, on emerging from water or glass after striking the surface at nearly the critical angle, appears to be coloured. Explain fully why this is so.

9. What is meant by the dispersion of light? How would you show that the dispersive power of carbon disulphide is greater than that of water?

10. White light is passed through two prisms whose refracting edges are at right angles. Describe, with the aid of a diagram, the nature and position of the resulting spectrum.

11. Write a short account of the experiments by means of which Newton supported his theory of the composite nature of white light.

12. What is meant by the chromatic aberration of a lens and how may it be eliminated?

13. When a convex lens is used to produce a real image on a screen the edges of the image are coloured, especially if the image is slightly out of focus. Explain this. Why is no such effect obtained when a concave mirror is used to produce the image?

14. Explain, giving exact distances, how you would set up a spectrometer given a narrow slit, a glass prism, two converging lenses of focal length 20 cm. and one of focal length 5 cm. Trace two rays through the apparatus.

15. Trace a single ray of white light, showing its dispersion, as it passes through two prisms in contact, one of crown glass and the other of flint glass of such refracting angles that dispersion is produced but no deviation.

16. Give a brief account of a method of investigating the heating effect of the various parts of the spectrum of sunlight and state the results you would expect.

17. Write a short account of the invisible spectrum of sunlight.

Chapter VIII

COLOUR

To what do bodies owe their colour, and how is the sensation of colour received by the eye?

Obtain a red filter, such as is used in theatres for making the spotlight throw a red beam. Place it in the path of a beam of light which is forming a spectrum. All of the spectrum will be wiped out except the red end.

This simple experiment is most instructive. It reveals to us that the filter owes its red colour to the fact that it absorbs from white light all colours except red. It does not dye all the white light red, otherwise the whole spectrum would be seen as red. It merely absorbs all light but the red.

The experiment may be repeated with filters of other colours. Indeed it is a good test of the purity of a filter. If a supposedly green filter wipes out all the spectrum except the green, and also some of the red, it is not a pure green filter since it allows some of the red to pass through.

Let us now consider the case of a red ribbon. A red ribbon in white light looks red; in the dark it looks black or invisible. What will be its appearance when placed in different parts of the spectrum? At the red end of the spectrum it looks red, but in the rest of the spectrum—in the yellow, green or blue—it looks black (or nearly so). This is due to the fact that it absorbs all the light that falls upon it except the red, which it sends to the eye. The light is absorbed as it passes through the red dye and the red light is reflected at the fibres of the material underneath. Thus the fibres previous to dyeing must be capable of reflecting any light which falls upon them, i.e. they must be approximately white. Red ink, for example, does not show up on black paper.

Another instructive experiment is to illuminate a dark room with monochromatic yellow sodium light, obtained by placing a small piece of rock salt on the gauze top of a Meker burner. Objects whose colours in white light are yellow or white, look yellow, and all other objects look black. A human face in this light looks ghastly.

The colour of an object, therefore, depends partly upon the light which falls upon it. Since an ordinary electric light bulb emits light in which there is a greater preponderance of red and yellow than sunlight (or alternatively in which there is not sufficient blue light) accurate colour matching in electric light is impossible. Large stores, therefore, provide for this purpose powerful "daylight" lamps, which are tinted blue to cut down the percentage of red and yellow light, and give out light of a composition similar to daylight. The Sheringham daylight lamp has a reflector painted a blue-green colour.

We may sum up by saying that the colour of an object is due to the fact that it absorbs light of all colours except its own, i.e. the colour that it sends to the eye in daylight (which we accept as our standard white light). In artificial light its appearance varies according to the nature of the light which falls upon it.

A white body absorbs no light, and hence assumes the colour of the light which falls upon it; a red body absorbs light of all colours but red; and a black body absorbs all the light.

It is worth while distinguishing here between body colour and surface colour. Thin gold foil appears yellow by reflected light (surface colour) and green when held between a lamp and the eye (body colour). The gold foil reflects yellow light and transmits green light. We have already pointed out that the red (body) colour of a ribbon is due to light of all colours but red being absorbed as it passes through the dye and the reflection of the red light at the fibres underneath. The transmission through and partial absorption by the "body" of a substance is an essential part of the mechanism of body colour.

Colour mixing by addition.

Let the light from three lanterns shine on to a screen so that the three light patches overlap. It is thus possible to examine the sensation the eye receives when light of three colours enters the eye simultaneously. We have already noted two other arrangements which may be used for this purpose: (i) Newton's colour disc, and (ii) his method of recombining by means of a lens either the whole of, or certain selected colours from, the spectrum.

By means of the three lanterns and suitable pure filters we can demonstrate the following facts:

1. Red + green + blue lights look white.
2. Red + green lights look yellow.

3. Red + blue lights look magenta (a blood-red colour, which takes its name from a battlefield in Switzerland).

4. Green + blue lights look peacock blue.

These facts can be represented very conveniently by means of a diagram called the colour triangle (see Fig. 114). The three colours, red, green and blue, called the *primary colours* are placed at the vertices of an equilateral triangle. Midway between the red and green is written yellow, since red and green light, when they enter the eye simultaneously, give the sensation of yellow. Peacock blue and magenta are placed between the green and blue and the blue and red, respectively. At the centre of the triangle is written white, since red, green and blue when entering the eye together give the sensation of white. We can see also that

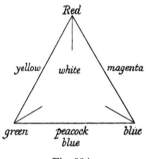

Fig. 114

1 part blue + 2 parts yellow will give white light,

since   1 part red + 1 part green gives 2 parts yellow.

The above are facts which anyone can verify for himself, by experiment. What may be deduced from these facts as regards the nature and operation of colour vision?

Colour vision.

The most significant fact which we have to face is that the sensation of white can be produced not only by all the colours of the spectrum together, but also by three single colours, red, green and blue. Further, it can be demonstrated that any colour sensation can be produced by blending these three colours in suitable proportions.

A theory has been put forward by Young and Helmholtz that in the eye there are three sets of nerves which are sensitive to red, green and violet light respectively. When these nerves are equally stimulated the sensation of white is experienced. When the red and green nerves are equally excited, yellow is seen, and so on; any colour sensation may be produced by the simultaneous excitation of these nerves in the correct proportional intensities.

The theory is not completely satisfactory. Anatomically there appears to be only one kind of nerve connected with colour vision in the retina. When pure monochromatic light of a colour other than primary enters the eye it stimulates according to the theory two or more sets of nerves. Thus pure monochromatic yellow is assumed to stimulate both the "red" and the "green" nerves. This does, however, explain the fact that the eye is a very non-selective colour receiver. When the eye receives the sensation of yellow it cannot differentiate between pure monochromatic yellow light such as is emitted by a sodium flame and a mixture of red and green light. The ear is much more sensitive in this respect. When two notes are sounded the ear can usually resolve them, and is hardly ever deceived into recording a single note blended of the two.

Colour blindness.

The Young-Helmholtz theory is supported by the phenomenon of colour blindness.

A red-colour blind person, as a rule, cannot distinguish red from a dull blue-green colour. The world appears to him, we believe, as it does to a normal person when viewed through a peacock-blue filter. The Young-Helmholtz theory explains the phenomenon by suggesting that the red nerves in the eyes of a colour blind person do not function. Hence when red light enters his eye he does not see a bright colour, but a dull blue-green owing to the green and blue nerves being very slightly stimulated. Occasionally the green or the blue nerves do not function, but red-colour blindness is by far the most common. It is believed that about one man in every twenty-five is colour blind, and that the defect is hereditary.

The phenomenon was discovered by John Dalton, the famous chemist, who is said to have found difficulty in picking out a red hunting jacket placed in a distant green field, and to have appeared on occasions, to the distress of his Quaker friends, in a sober coat and breeches and red stockings.

Colour blindness is not a very great handicap except to men in certain professions, notably engine drivers. An engine driver is subjected, at the outset of his career, to very rigorous colour tests, such as the sorting out of wools or beads of many subtle shades, and distinguishing between lights of different colours.

Fatigue colour.

Another interesting phenomenon, that of fatigue colour, lends support to the Young-Helmholtz theory.

If you look for a short time at an intense source of red light and then transfer your gaze immediately to a brightly illuminated sheet of white paper, you will see a bluey-green image of the source. Whatever the colour of the original source, you see the complementary colour (see p. 116) on looking at a white background.

This is explained by assuming that the red nerves are fatigued by looking at an intense source of red light. On looking at a white object all the nerves are excited, but since in that part of the retina where the image of the red source fell the red nerves are fatigued, this area of the retina will record a peacock-blue colour.

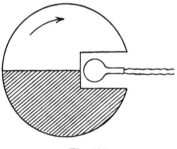

Fig. 115

A very striking experiment may be set up to demonstrate the phenomenon. Place a red lamp behind a large disc of cardboard one half of which is painted white and the other black, and from which a portion has been cut as in Fig. 115.

Rotate the disc at the rate of about 2 or 3 rev. per sec. in the direction shown in the figure. The red lamp will appear to be green.

This experiment is not capable of an entirely simple explanation. But the eye, after being stimulated by the red lamp, is immediately afterwards stimulated by the white half of the disc, and the fatigue colour is apparently more powerful than the original stimulation. For the experiment to be successful the disc must be brightly illuminated.

Colour mixing by subtraction.

If two filters, red and green for example, are placed in front of the same lantern, each will extract from the light all colours but its own. They will therefore effectively block all light (if they are pure filters), since the red filter absorbs all light but the red, and the green filter absorbs the red.

Suppose three circular filters are made to overlap as in Fig. 116. If 1, 2 and 3 are red, green and blue, the three primary colours, as they are called, then 4, 5, 6 and 7 should all be black.

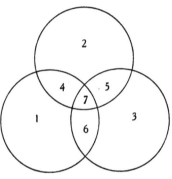

Fig. 116

But now suppose that 1, 2, 3 are the three "secondaries", yellow, magenta and peacock blue, respectively. Then 4 will be red, 5 blue, 6 green, and 7 black. The explanation is as follows. Where 1 and 2 overlap, i.e. 4, the light which is common to yellow and magenta, namely red, will be allowed to pass. A similar argument applies to 5 and 6. At 7 the three filters overlap, and since they allow no common colour to pass, 7 will be black. This may be called colour mixing by subtraction.

Three-colour printing is done on this principle. Inks whose colours are approximately the three secondaries are used. When made to overlap in pairs, they produce three more colours, the three primaries. Thus printing in six colours is possible.

The production of colours by mixing paints or pigments is also a process of colour subtraction. When suitable blue and yellow lights are mixed they produce white since both colours enter the eye, and the process is one of addition. When however blue and yellow paints are mixed they produce green paint. If the paints were pure blue and yellow, when mixed they would produce black paint. However, the blue paint absorbs light of all colours except blue and a little violet and green, its neighbours in the spectrum. Similarly yellow paint absorbs light of all colours except yellow and a little orange and green. Thus blue and yellow mixed together absorb all light except green (which is then reflected by the white paper beneath)—a process of subtraction. It is clear that the resulting green cannot be so bright a colour as the original yellow and blue. Hence artists usually prefer to use a green pigment rather than mix yellow and blue.

Colour due to scattering.

A crystal of copper sulphate is blue, but when ground to a powder it appears white. This is due to the fact that light cannot penetrate into the powder but is scattered in all directions at the surface, and therefore little or no light is absorbed.

Now the constituents of white light are scattered to a different extent by very small particles. The particles of powdered copper sulphate referred to above are comparatively large and scatter all the light. The molecules comprising the atmosphere, however, are very minute and they scatter only the shortest wave-lengths in white light, i.e. the blue. This is the explanation of the blue colour of the sky. The blue rays in the light from the sun on reaching the atmosphere are scattered in all directions, and hence, in whatever direction one looks at the sky, it appears blue. The sun itself appears yellow instead of white, since sunlight on arrival at the eye has lost part of its blue constituents. Some of the scattering is caused by fine dust particles suspended in the atmosphere. Above 3000 ft., the height of the earth's dust layer, the sky appears a darker blue since the air molecules scatter only the blue light of shortest wave-length.

Wisps of smoke from the end of a burning cigarette are a bright blue colour, but that emitted from the mouth of the smoker is grey. The carbon particles of the smoke are coated with water vapour from the mouth of the smoker and hence become larger. They scatter, therefore, light of longer wave-length as well as the blue.

The gold and red colours of the sunset are caused by the scattering of the blue and green rays of sunlight by the dust particles in the atmosphere. When the sun is near the horizon its light passes through a greater thickness of atmosphere than when it is higher in the sky. Consequently more scattering takes place and it looks red. After the tremendous eruption in 1883 of the volcano Krakatoa, which hurled great clouds of dust into the atmosphere, magnificent sunsets were seen for many months.

It has been proved recently by Raman that the blue colour of the sea is due in part to the scattering of light by the water molecules; the blue colour is partly due also to reflection from the sky. Shallow water looks green owing to the scattering of light of longer wave-length by suspended sand particles and also to the reflection of yellow light by the sand.

Here again in the phenomenon of colour produced by the scattering of light we see that the colour is originally resident in the white light. The white light is split up by selective scattering and only light of certain colours reaches the eye.

Infra-red photography.

Owing to their longer wave-length, infra-red rays are less scattered than visible rays and they can penetrate haze more easily. They are therefore eminently suitable for distance photography. In recent years photographic plates have been prepared which are sensitive to infra-red rays.

Plate VIII, facing p. 129, shows two photographs, one taken with an infra-red filter (which admits only infra-red rays into the camera) and a plate sensitised to infra-red radiation, and one taken in the ordinary way. In the former the foliage looks white, almost as though it were covered with snow. This is due to the fact that chlorophyll, the colouring matter of leaves, does not absorb the red and infra-red rays and reflects them strongly into the camera.

SUMMARY

The colour of a body is due to the fact that it absorbs light of all colours but its own, which it sends to the eye.

Red, green and violet light, on entering the eye simultaneously give the sensation of white. According to the Young-Helmholtz theory of colour vision there are three sets of nerves in the eye which give rise to these three primary colour sensations and all colours are caused by their simultaneous stimulation in varying degrees. The theory is supported by the phenomena of colour blindness and fatigue colour.

Blue light + yellow light → white light.

Blue paint + yellow paint → green paint.

The former is a process of colour mixing by addition and the latter by subtraction.

Colour may be produced by the scattering of light.

QUESTIONS

1. What colour will (*a*) a white, (*b*) a blue, (*c*) a red, object appear to be when looked at through red glass? Explain.

2. If yellow and blue paints are mixed they produce green paint. If, however, yellow and blue lights are shone together on to a screen they produce white light. Explain fully.

3. How do the yellow colours of a sodium flame and a buttercup differ in nature and origin?

4. A match-box lid has green lettering on a red background. Describe and explain its appearance when held (a) in the red, (b) in the green part of the spectrum. (C.)

5. Describe two experiments showing the composite nature of white light.

A checkerboard of orange and blue squares is examined (i) in white light, (ii) in red light, and is photographed. Describe the appearance of the checkerboard in the two lights and in the photograph. (O. & C.)

6. Explain why the light from the setting sun is red.

7. What is the appearance of a picture of red and green paint when illuminated with red and then with yellow light? (C.)

8. Explain: Many substances, such as coloured glass, which are coloured when in large pieces, appear white after they have been crushed to a very fine powder. (O. & C.)

9. What do you understand by the terms *primary colour* and *complementary colour*?

Describe an experiment to show that two suitably coloured lights focused on one spot produce white light. Can you suggest any means of deciding whether this white light is different from ordinary white light? (O.)

10. Explain why snow is white while ice is colourless and clear. Describe and explain the effect produced in the appearance of snow by wetting it.

11. Why is colour matching difficult in artificial light? What colours should be hardest to match in this light?

12. A beam of sunlight from a pinhole traverses a prism made of purple glass, transmitting only red and blue rays. Explain the appearance of the beam after passage through the prism.

A second similar prism, but of clear glass, and inverted with respect to the first, is placed behind the first prism. Explain the effects produced.

If in each of these cases the rays were received upon a piece of red paper, what would be the appearance of the paper? (O.)

13. On what does the apparent colour of an object depend? Explain carefully.

14. Write a critical account of the Young-Helmholtz theory of colour vision. What phenomena support the theory and what are its weaknesses?

15. Explain:

(*a*) A disc marked with blue and yellow sectors appears nearly white when it is spun.

(*b*) White light appears green when it passes through inferior blue and yellow glass.

(*c*) Red ink which has dried on a pen nib appears green.

16. Is the penetrating power of the light from a motor-car head-lamp increased in fog by placing a red filter over the lamp? Explain.

17. Explain why the smoke from a cottage chimney appears blue when viewed against a dark background of trees, but appears reddish brown when viewed against the bright background of the sky.

Chapter IX

PHOTOMETRY

The study of the intensity of light is called photometry.

What is it precisely that causes a beam of light from a searchlight to be more intense than a beam from a pocket electric torch? There is a greater quantity of light streaming from the searchlight per second than from the torch. We have seen, in Chapter I, that light is a form of energy. The searchlight is therefore emitting light energy at a greater rate than the torch.

The fundamental unit of energy is the erg, and it is possible to measure light energy in ergs by allowing it to fall upon a black body and finding its heating effect (1 calorie = 4·2 × 10⁷ ergs). The visible light energy must first be separated from the invisible infra-red radiation. Indeed only 2 per cent. of the energy radiated by a candle is in the form of light.

Since, however, we are chiefly concerned with the luminous rather than the heating effect of light, most measurements in photometry are based, not upon the erg, but upon a standard source of light.

The standard source.

The first standard chosen was the British Standard Candle, a sperm candle, weighing six to the pound and burning at the rate of 120 grains per hour. This standard is not accurate and has been superseded, but the unit in which illuminating power is measured is still called the *candle-power.*

A special lamp, constructed to accurate specifications, and burning pentane vapour, called the Vernon Harcourt Pentane Lamp, is now used in this country as the ultimate standard. Its illuminating power is taken as 10 candle-power. In Germany, the Hefner lamp, which burns amyl acetate, is employed as the standard, and the unit used is the hefner, which is 0·9 candle-power.

In practice, for the sake of convenience, subsidiary electric lamp standards are used. They must be calibrated against a

Vernon Harcourt pentane lamp at intervals. Care must be taken
always to use the light emitted by such a lamp in the particular
direction employed when calibrating it and also to supply the
correct voltage to the lamp after first well seasoning it by passing
a current larger than normal.

Luminosity (or Illuminating power).

The luminosity of a source (in candle–power)

$$= \frac{\textbf{Rate of emission of light by the source}}{\textbf{Rate of emission of light by a standard candle}}.$$

The standard candle here referred to is the theoretical candle
of one-tenth the power of a Vernon Harcourt lamp.

If the total light emitted in all directions is compared with the
total light emitted by a standard candle, the result is called the
mean spherical candle-power.

The photo-electric photometer.

It is impossible to estimate the comparative luminosities of
two sources of light from the sensations of brightness which they
produce in the eye. The eye is sensitive to an enormous range of
intensities—full sunlight, for instance, is half a million times
more intense than moonlight—but the sensation of brightness is

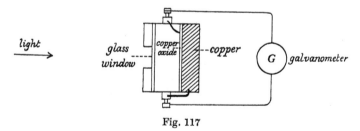

Fig. 117

not proportional to the intensity of the light. Thus a lamp of
16 candle-power appears only $2\frac{3}{4}$ times as bright as a candle. An
instrument for comparing luminosities is termed a *photometer.*

The most straightforward type of photometer is a photo-
electric cell. On p. 4 we explained that when light falls on
certain metals the latter emit electrons. A similar effect occurs
with a deposit of copper oxide on a copper plate, and the electrons

emitted by the copper oxide are gained by the copper plate. When the circuit is completed by joining the copper oxide with wires to a sensitive galvanometer and thence to the copper again (see Fig. 117), the electrons flow round the circuit, constituting an electric current, which may be measured by the galvanometer. (No auxiliary battery is required with this type of cell and the current may be as large as 1 milliampere.)

Now although, as we explained on p. 4, the velocity of the electrons does not depend on the intensity of the light, their number, and hence the magnitude of the current, is proportional

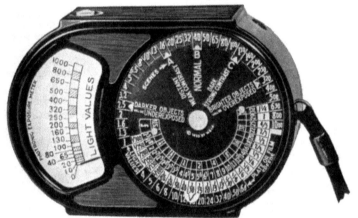

By courtesy of the Weston Electrical Instrument Co. Ltd.

Fig. 118. An exposure meter which measures the intensity, or "light value", of the light falling on it by means of a photo-electric cell (aperture at the back). The movable dial enables this intensity, as indicated by the pointer, to be translated into terms of exposure for a given stop and speed of plate.

to the light intensity. Thus a photo-electric cell connected to a galvanometer can be used as a direct-reading instrument for measuring the intensity of light.

Experiments with the photo-electric cell.

1. *Preliminary experiment to show that the cell response is proportional to the amount of light falling on it.*

Place a lamp some distance in front of the cell (e.g. a 40-watt opal lamp at about 2 metres), and note the deflection of the galvanometer. Place another lamp beside the first (arranging it as far as possible so that the lamps are similarly orientated with respect to the cell) and note that the deflection is doubled. Repeat with three, four, etc. lamps (see Fig. 119). It is advisable to cover the table with *lamps* green baize during these experiments to prevent stray reflected light from the polished table top reaching the cell.

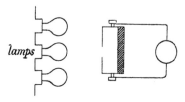

Fig. 119. The distance between the lamps and the photo-electric cell is much greater than is shown in this diagram.

2. *Comparison of the luminosities of two lamps.*

Place a standard lamp of specified luminosity at a noted distance from the cell and read the deflection of the galvanometer. Replace the standard lamp by the other lamp of unknown luminosity, at the same distance, and note the new deflection. The ratio of the deflections is equal to the ratio of the luminosities. This method is exactly analogous to the use of an ungraduated spring balance to compare weights.

3. *Investigation of the light distribution round a lamp.*

Move the cell round the lamp at a fixed distance a noted number of degrees at a time, and read the galvanometer deflections for each position.

Fig. 120 represents the light distribution round (*a*) a 40-watt cage-filament transparent vacuum lamp, and (*b*) a 40-watt coiled-coil filament opal gas-filled lamp. The caps of the lamps may be regarded as situated at points corresponding to *O*. The distances of the curves from *O* represent the intensities of the light distribution. It will be seen that the transparent lamp gives out far more light sideways than downwards, whereas the opal lamp gives out light comparatively uniformly in all directions, except, of course, in the direction of its cap.

These curves were obtained by keeping the cell fixed, and making the lamp rotate slowly by clockwork about its middle point. A narrow beam of light (from a separate source) was reflected at the galvanometer mirror and, acting as a deflection pointer, fell on photographic paper, which rotated in a vertical plane at the same speed and about the same axis as the lamp. The undeflected spot of light fell on the paper at O, its centre of rotation, and moved sideways as the deflection altered.

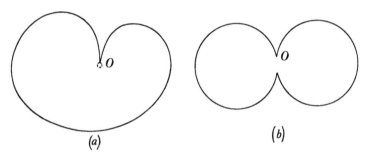

(a) (b)

Fig. 120

4. *Determination of the way in which the intensity of the light from a point source falls off with the distance from the source.*

Place a motor-car headlamp (with a small filament) at a convenient distance from the cell. Note the deflection. Double the distance of the lamp from the cell: the deflection is now approximately one-quarter of its original value. Treble the distance: the deflection is reduced to one-ninth of its original value.

This experiment demonstrates the truth of the following law.

The inverse square law.

The intensity of illumination due to a point source of light varies inversely as the square of the distance from it,

$$\text{i.e.} \quad I \propto \frac{1}{d^2}.$$

We may define the **intensity of illumination** of a surface as the **quantity of light falling on unit area per sec.**

In Fig. 121 light from a point source S falls upon the area $ABCD$. Since light travels in straight lines the same quantity of light would fall upon the larger area $EFGH$ if $ABCD$ were removed. Suppose $EFGH$ is twice as far from S as $ABCD$. It is clear from similar triangles that $EF = 2AB$ and $FG = 2BC$.

Hence the area of *EFGH* is four times the area of *ABCD*. Since the same quantity of light falls on both surfaces the intensity at *EFGH* is only $\frac{1}{4}$ $\left(=\frac{1}{2^2}\right)$ that at *ABCD*. Similarly, the intensity at *KLMN*, if $SK=3SA$, is $\frac{1}{9}$ $\left(=\frac{1}{3^2}\right)$ that at *ABCD*. (Strictly, in order to be uniformly illuminated, each surface should be not plane, but part of the surface of a sphere with *S* as centre.)

We have defined intensity of illumination as the quantity of light falling on unit area per sec. *Unit quantity of light* is taken as *that falling on unit area* (e.g. 1 sq. ft.) *at unit distance* (e.g. 1 ft.)

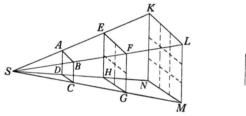

Fig. 121

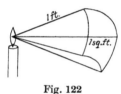

Fig. 122

from a standard candle, held perpendicular to the light. It is called 1 *lumen*. Each point on the area must be equidistant from the candle, and the area must therefore be part of a sphere with the candle as centre (see Fig. 122).

Thus if a point source, of candle-power *c*, produces an intensity of illumination *I*, at a surface distant *d* ft. away, and at right angles to the light,

$$I = \frac{c}{d^2}.$$

If the surface is inclined at an angle θ to the perpendicular to the light, then

$$I = \frac{c}{d^2} \cos \theta.$$

This can be proved as follows:

In Fig. 123 the quantity of light *Q* falling on *AB*, a surface held obliquely to light from *S*, is equal to that falling on *A'B'*, a surface at right angles to the light.

But $\qquad\qquad A'B' = AB \cos \theta.$

If I and I' are the intensities of illumination at AB and $A'B'$ respectively,

$$I = \frac{Q}{AB}, \qquad I' = \frac{Q}{AB'} = \frac{Q}{AB \cos \theta}.$$

$$\therefore \quad I = I' \cos \theta = \frac{c}{d^2} \cos \theta.$$

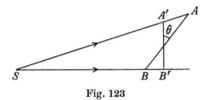

Fig. 123

Inverse square law photometers.

The luminosities of two sources of light may be compared by adjusting the distances of the sources from a surface until they give equal illumination, and then applying the inverse square law. Thus if c_1 and c_2 are the candle-powers of the two sources, and d_1 and d_2 respectively their distances from the surface when they give equal illumination,

$$\frac{c_1}{d_1{}^2} = \frac{c_2}{d_2{}^2}.$$

The Bunsen grease-spot photometer consists of a grease-spot in a sheet of paper. The sources to be compared are placed on either side of the grease-spot and their distances adjusted until the grease-spot appears neither darker nor lighter than the paper. The intensities of illumination produced by the two lamps are then equal.

In Rumford's shadow photometer, the two shadows of a rod cast on a screen by the two sources, placed on the same side of the screen, are made equally dark by adjusting the positions of the sources. Since each shadow is illuminated by the source which is not casting it, the intensities of illumination at the screen due to the two sources are equal.

Bunsen's and Rumford's photometers are not accurate and are of historical interest only.

The most accurate of the simple photometers, suitable for use in a school laboratory, is *Joly's paraffin-wax photometer*. It consists of two slabs of paraffin-wax with a sheet of tinfoil between (see Fig. 124). The wax is viewed from the side and the lamps are adjusted until the two slabs look equally bright.

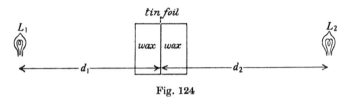

Fig. 124

Measurement of intensity of illumination.

Intensity of illumination is measured in **foot candles** or **metre candles**. A surface has an **intensity of illumination of 1 foot candle when placed 1 ft. away from a standard candle and at right angles to the light** (i.e. it is receiving light at the rate of 1 lumen per sq. ft. per sec.).

An instrument called a foot-candle meter, similar in operation to a grease-spot photometer, is used to measure intensity of illumination direct. The interior is shown in Fig. 125. A row of

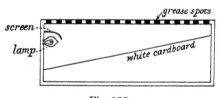

Fig. 125

small grease-spots on paper, fitted in a slot in the top of a box, is illuminated from below by a small lamp, the light from which is reflected upwards by a tilted sheet of white cardboard. The grease-spots are shielded from direct light from the lamp by means of a small screen. When the instrument is in place where the intensity of illumination is required, say on a desk in a classroom, the grease-spots at one end of the scale will look bright and those at the other end will look dark (see Fig. 126). Intermediately there will be a grease-spot which is neither brighter nor darker than the surrounding white paper. This grease-spot is equally illuminated from above as from below. Its position on the scale gives the required reading in foot candles.

The instrument is calibrated with an electric lamp whose exact candle-power has been determined at the National Physical Laboratory by comparison with a Vernon Harcourt lamp. This electric lamp is placed at different distances from the grease-spots and the intensity of illumination it produces can be calculated from the formula $I = \dfrac{c}{d^2}$. The grease-spot which appears the same brightness as its surroundings is given the calculated value in each case.

Fig. 126. The grease-spots and scale of the foot-candle meter shown in Fig. 125. The reading here is about 8 foot candles. (The lamp inside the instrument is on the right-hand side of this picture.)

Care must be taken to ensure that the lamp inside the instrument always receives the correct voltage: for unless the illuminating power of this lamp is kept accurately constant the grease-spot scale will be completely unreliable. Consequently a voltmeter and potentiometer are incorporated in the instrument.

Illumination.

The study of the illumination of rooms and buildings is an important branch of applied physics.

In schools and offices the best daylight illumination is believed to be about 100 foot candles, and a satisfactory intensity of artificial illumination is 5 foot candles. Electric lamps are not rated according to their candle-power but by the rate at which they use up electric energy, e.g. 40 watt or 100 watt. A gas-filled lamp gives approximately 1 c.p. per $1\frac{1}{4}$ watts. Thus a 40-watt gas-filled lamp has a candle-power of $\dfrac{40}{1\frac{1}{4}} = 32$. Such a lamp (if unassisted by reflections from walls or a lamp reflector) produces, at a distance of 4 ft., an intensity of illumination of approximately $\dfrac{32}{4^2} = 2$ foot candles.

Good reflecting surfaces such as walls and ceilings play an important part in illumination. In engineering shops, where the surfaces absorb most of the light that falls upon them, lamps of greater power are required than in a class-room where the ceiling is white and the walls are a light colour. The walls and ceiling of the class-room add their quota to the general illumination by reflecting back a large percentage of the light that falls upon them.

A modern method of illumination is indirect lighting by a ceiling lit by concealed lamps which throw their light upwards. Now the inverse square law does not hold for a source with a large area—such as a ceiling. Indeed, it can be shown mathematically that a uniform source of infinite area produces an intensity of illumination which is the same at all distances. The method of indirect lighting, therefore, gives a uniform illumination throughout the room. On the other hand, entirely indirect lighting is not desirable owing to the almost complete absence of shadows and therefore of relief and moulding of solid objects.

It has been found that a high illumination intensity in a factory results in rapid work. Hence good lighting is an economy in the long run.

The following tables are of interest:

Illuminating powers.

	Candle-power
Candle	1
40-watt electric lamp (gas-filled)	30
Electric arc	1000–2000
Eddystone lighthouse lamp	80,000
Sun	3×10^{27}

Intensities of illumination.

	Foot candles
Full sunlight	7000–10,000
Room in daylight	30–40
Room in artificial light	1–3
Full moonlight	$\frac{1}{100} - \frac{1}{50}$

SUMMARY

The theoretical standard source of light is the standard candle.

Luminosity or illuminating power of a source of light

$$= \frac{\textbf{Rate of emission of light by the source}}{\textbf{Rate of emission of light by a standard candle}}.$$

The luminosity of two sources may be compared by a photo-electric photometer.

Unit quantity of light, 1 lumen, is the light falling on unit area at unit distance from a standard candle held perpendicular to the light.

The intensity of illumination of a surface is the quantity of light falling on unit area per sec.

Inverse square law.

The intensity of illumination due to a point source of light varies inversely as the square of the distance from it,

$$\text{i.e.} \quad I \propto \frac{1}{d^2}.$$

The luminosities of two sources of light may be compared by inverse square law photometers such as those of Bunsen, Rumford and Joly.

The intensity of illumination of a surface may be measured by a foot-candle meter.

QUESTIONS

1. How would you arrange to compare the illuminating powers of two small electric lights by means of a shadow photometer; what measurements would you take; how would the calculation be made; and what is the main principle on which the method depends?

2. Explain the action of a grease-spot photometer. Define the term *foot candle.*

Lamps of 16 c.p. and x c.p. are placed 50 in. apart on a bench. A screen held vertically between the lamps is illuminated equally by both when it is 22 in. from the 16 c.p. lamp. What is the candle-power of the other lamp?

3. A nominal 16 c.p. incandescent electric bulb gives the same intensity of illumination of a screen 60 cm. away as a standard 10 c.p. lamp at 50 cm. What is its true candle-power?

4. Explain carefully why you would expect the intensity of illumination of a screen, illuminated by a small light source, to vary inversely with the square of its distance from the source.

If a photographic print can be made with 4 sec. exposure at a distance of 4 ft. from a 32 c.p. lamp, what exposure will be required if the negative is held at 2 ft. from a 16 c.p. lamp? (O. & C.)

5. Explain the terms: *illuminating power of a source of light; illumination of a surface.* In what units may they be measured?

A 30 c.p. lamp at 4 ft. distance from a surface is replaced by a 50 c.p. lamp at $4\frac{1}{2}$ ft. distance. Compare the illumination of the surface in the two cases. (L.)

6. Two lamps of candle-power 1 and 16 respectively are set up 3 ft. apart. Find where a screen must be placed between them and on the line joining them to be equally illuminated by the two lamps.

(O.)

7. On one side of a screen are placed a 4 c.p. lamp at a distance of 20 in. and a 3 c.p. lamp at a distance of 30 in. What must be the candle-power of a single lamp to produce equal illumination on the screen at a distance of 30 in.? (O.)

8. Two lamps of 10 and 15 c.p. are arranged at distances of 12 and 16 in. respectively from the screen of a shadow photometer in such positions that only one shadow is formed. How far from the screen must a lamp of 20 c.p. be placed in order to produce a shadow equally intense?

9. Two lamps produce equal illuminations on the two sides of a photometer when placed at distances of 40 and 50 cm. When a sheet of glass is put in front of the stronger lamp, the weaker lamp has to be moved 4 cm. farther away to restore equality of illumination. What percentage of the light is stopped by the glass? (O. & C.)

10. Define the terms *reflect, emit, absorb.* Describe an experiment by which one might compare the reflecting powers of different surfaces for white light. (O.)

11. Would you expect the intensity of the light in a searchlight beam to vary inversely as the square of the distance from the source? Give your reasons.

12. What is the illumination in foot candles produced by a 60-watt lamp, rated at 1·2 watts per candle-power at a distance of 5 ft.?

13. If an intensity of illumination of 3 foot candles is required for reading, how far from the book must a 30 c.p. reading lamp be placed (assuming the room to be dark and ignoring reflection from the lamp shade)?

14. Find the rate at which light is emitted, in lumens per sec., by a lamp of 60 c.p.

15. A horizontal footpath is illuminated by a lamp fixed at a height of 12 ft. above the ground. Compare the intensity of illumination of the path immediately below the lamp with that at a point 16 ft. farther along the path. (L.)

16. A 600 c.p. lamp is suspended at a height of 5 ft. above a large table. Calculate the illumination in foot candles at points on the table distant 5, 6, 8, 10, 12 and 15 ft. respectively from the lamp.

Exhibit your results in the form of a curve.

17. How many times is the intensity of illumination at a point distant 18 in. from a 24 c.p. lamp increased when a converging lens of focal length 5 in. and aperture 1 in. is placed between them, 10 in. from the lamp?

Chapter X

MICROSCOPES AND TELESCOPES

The function of microscopes and telescopes is to enable the eye to see more clearly objects which are very small or very distant (*micro*—small, *tele*—far, *scopein*—I see).

Magnifying glass or simple microscope.

The magnifying glass consists of a converging lens, which is used to produce a virtual, erect and magnified image (see Fig. 59, p. 60). The lens must be held at a shorter distance than its focal length from the object to be viewed, otherwise an inverted, real image is formed. It is evident from the figure that the nearer F_1 is to the lens, i.e. the shorter the focal length, the greater is the magnification.

Such lenses are often used for reading small print, or for reading the vernier on a fine scale. Industrially, they are used for counting the number of threads to the inch in cloth in order to estimate the cost of production.

The compound microscope.

There is a limit below which the focal length of a lens cannot be reduced, owing to the distortion of the image.

In order to obtain high magnification, therefore, a compound microscope is used. The compound microscope consists, essentially, of two converging lenses, both of short focal length. The first lens, called the objective, produces a real, highly magnified image, and the second lens, called the eyepiece, behaves as an ordinary magnifying glass and magnifies this image.

Fig. 127 shows the action of the instrument. The objective forms a real image, I_1, of the object, O. O must therefore be farther away from the objective than its focal length. I_1, on the other hand, must be nearer to the eyepiece than its focal length, since the eyepiece forms a virtual image I_2 of I_1. Construction lines, marked ····· are drawn from I_1 to obtain the actual position of I_2; when this position is known the two rays from the top of O

can be continued through the eyepiece. The construction lines represent the usual rays which would be drawn if I_1 were the original object. Actually, of course, all rays must start from O. Note also that in the diagram only half the object has been drawn.

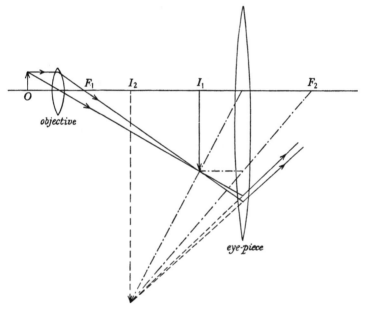

Fig. 127. The compound microscope.

You should set up two short focus convex lenses to act as a compound microscope. You will notice the following defects: (1) great distortion of the image, called spherical aberration; (2) the image is slightly coloured—called chromatic aberration; (3) the field of view is small.

These defects are eliminated by making the objective and eyepiece of several lenses.

Objectives are made of very short focal length $\frac{2}{3}$ in., $\frac{1}{6}$ in. or even $\frac{1}{12}$ in., so that the length of the instrument can be kept small.

The microscope shown in Fig. 128 has two objectives of focal lengths $\frac{2}{3}$ in. and $\frac{1}{6}$ in. The eyepiece produces a maximum magnification of 6, written ×6. Using the first objective, the magnification produced by the instrument is 64 and using the second objective, 295. Thus the objectives must produce magnifications of $\frac{64}{6} = 10$ approx., and $\frac{295}{6} = 49$ approx., respectively. The microscope is focused by moving the instrument as a whole: the eyepiece and objective do not move relative to each other.

Magnifications of 2000 (sometimes written 2000 diameters) are possible for visual use, and for photographing very small objects 5000 diameters have been used.

Strong illumination is essential, since the final image is so much larger than the object, and therefore much less bright. A mirror is used to reflect light on or through the object (see Fig. 128) and sometimes an arrangement of lenses, called a condenser. A bent glass rod illuminator is also used (see p. 45).

Is there any limit to the magnification that can be obtained with a compound microscope? The answer is "yes", owing to the nature of light. Bodies smaller than the wavelength of light cannot reflect light,

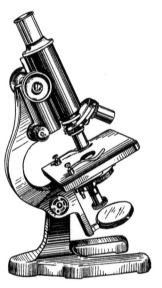

Fig. 128. Compound microscope.

just as a pebble is powerless to reflect the waves of the sea.

However, very tiny particles can be seen as points of light if a powerful beam of light is shone on to them at right angles to the direction in which they are viewed. The tiny particles diffract the light, i.e. cause it to bend in all directions. Such an arrangement is known as an ultra-microscope and by its aid objects with a diameter as small as $\frac{1}{25}$ of a millionth of an inch can be detected (but their true shape is not shown).

The astronomical telescope.

The astronomical telescope consists, like a compound microscope, of a converging objective and a converging eyepiece.

A telescope, however, is used for viewing distant objects whereas a microscope is used for viewing objects which are close at hand. The function of the objective of a telescope is, therefore, to form a real image of the distant object, as large as possible, but necessarily much smaller than the object. The eyepiece acts as a magnifying glass, and magnifies the real image formed by the objective.

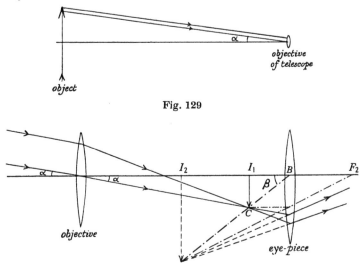

Fig. 129

Fig. 130. Astronomical telescope.

Fig. 130 shows the action of an astronomical telescope. The object is so large and so distant that it cannot be put in the figure. We must content ourselves with a parallel beam drawn from the top of the object (see Fig. 129).

In Fig. 130 I_1 represents the real image formed by the objective, and I_2 the virtual image formed by the eyepiece. Note that the final image formed by this telescope is inverted.

Since the object is, for all practical purposes, at infinity, the image I_1 is formed in the focal plane of the objective. Thus in order that I_1 shall be large, the focal length of the objective must be large, and this entails making the length of the telescope large also. A powerful astronomical telescope must, therefore, consist of (1) an objective of long focal length, (2) an eyepiece of short focal length.

The eyepiece of the telescope can be moved in and out but the distance between I_1 and the eyepiece must never be greater than the focal length of the latter, otherwise a virtual image will not be formed. When the eyepiece is moved so that I_1 is at a distance from it exactly equal to its focal length, the final image will be formed at infinity (see Fig. 131). The telescope is then said to be *in normal adjustment.* The distance between objective and eyepiece, in this case, is equal to the sum of their focal lengths. When looking through the telescope for long periods it is desirable to set it in normal adjustment in order to prevent eye-strain.

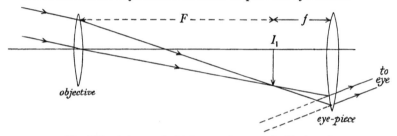

Fig. 131. Astronomical telescope in normal adjustment.

Magnifying power.

The apparent size of an object depends on its distance from the eye and is proportional to the angle subtended at the eye by the object (see Fig. 132). A sixpence held near to the eye looks larger than the moon since it subtends a larger angle at the eye than the moon.

When using a telescope it is the increase in the *apparent* size of the image that matters, and hence a new concept, *magnifying power*, is used instead of magnification. Magnification is the ratio of the actual sizes of the image and object, but magnifying power is the ratio of their apparent sizes.

The *magnifying power of a telescope*

$$= \frac{\text{Apparent size of image}}{\text{Apparent size of object}}$$

$$= \frac{\text{Angle subtended at eye by image}}{\text{Angle subtended at eye by object}}.$$

It can be shown that, when the astronomical telescope is in normal adjustment,

$$\text{Magnifying power} = \frac{\text{Focal length of objective}}{\text{Focal length of eyepiece}}.$$

In Fig. 130 the angles subtended at the eye by the object and image are α and β respectively.

$$\therefore \text{Magnifying power} = \beta/\alpha$$
$$= \frac{I_1 C/BI_1}{I_1 C/AI_1}$$
$$= \frac{AI_1}{BI_1}.$$

(Since α and β are small they are equal to $\tan \alpha$ and $\tan \beta$, approx.)

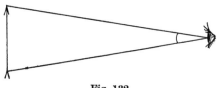

Fig. 132

When the telescope is in normal adjustment

$$\text{Magnifying power} = \frac{F}{f},$$

where F = focal length of the objective, and f = focal length of the eyepiece.

It will be seen that there is a slight increase in magnifying power as the eyepiece is moved in from the position of normal adjustment, since BI_1 is thereby reduced.

The largest refracting telescope in the world is the Yerkes telescope in the U.S.A. (see Figs. 133, 134). This telescope has an objective with a focal length of about 62 ft. It possesses several eyepieces of different powers, the most powerful having as short a focal length as $\frac{1}{4}$ in.

$$\text{Magnifying power of the telescope} = \frac{62}{1/48} \simeq 3000.$$

Every telescope has several eyepieces of different powers. The highest power is not always used because of the loss of brightness.

Fig. 133. The largest refracting telescope in the world, at the Yerkes Observatory, U.S.A.: the objective has an aperture of 40 in. The floor, which can be raised or lowered to accommodate the observer, is here shown in its lowest position (see also Fig. 134).

Fig. 134. The eye-end of the 40 in. Yerkes telescope
(see also Fig. 133).

The terrestrial telescope.

The astronomical telescope is unsuitable for terrestrial purposes since it makes all objects appear upside down. The defect can be remedied by inserting a converging "erecting" lens. This lens is most conveniently inserted at a distance $2f$ (where f is its focal length) from the real inverted image formed by the objective; it will then form a real, erect, image at a distance $2f$ on the other side. In Fig. 135 the position of the successive images is determined by considering each image as an object on its own, and drawing the usual pair of rays parallel to the axis and

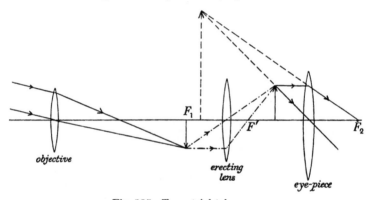

Fig. 135. Terrestrial telescope.

through the optical centre of the lens. This is permissible for construction purposes, but does not show the actual path of the rays, which, starting from the object, reach the eye, and enable the final image to be seen.

The drawback of the terrestrial telescope is its length. It must be longer than the astronomical telescope by at least $4f$, where f is the focal length of the erecting lens.

Prism binoculars.

Instead of using an erecting lens, the image formed by an astronomical telescope may be righted by means of prisms. This method is used in prism binoculars. The prisms reflect the light backwards and forwards, causing it to follow a zigzag path, and thus enable the binoculars to be made quite short in length (see Fig. 136). The prisms are right-angled, and one of them is standing up with its triangular section vertical, while the other is lying down with its triangular section horizontal. The first prism rights the image longitudinally, and the second laterally. There are two telescopes side by side, enabling both eyes to be used: hence the term, *binoculars.*

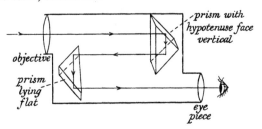

Fig. 136. Prism binoculars.

The Galilean telescope.

Another form of telescope, invented by Galileo, has a converging objective and a diverging eyepiece. The diverging eyepiece is used as a magnifying glass by giving it a virtual object to

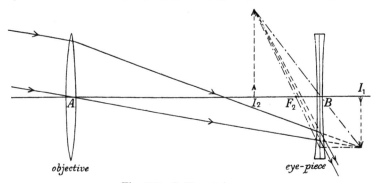

Fig. 137. Galilean telescope.

magnify. This is done by causing the objective to form a real image beyond the eyepiece. In Fig. 137 I_1 is the image which would be formed by the objective in the absence of the eyepiece, and I_2 is the image formed by the eyepiece of the virtual object I_1.

The advantage of this telescope is that the final image is erect and that the instrument is short $(F-f)$. It has the disadvantage of giving only a narrow field of view owing to the rays bending away from, instead of towards, the axis as they leave the eyepiece. Thus many of the rays will not enter the pupil of the eye. The Galilean telescope may be used for an opera glass, but is not suitable for the high magnifying powers required in astronomical observations, since the field of view becomes so small.

We will leave it as an exercise for the student to show that, for a Galilean telescope (see Fig. 137),

$$\text{Magnifying power} = \frac{AI_1}{BI_1}.$$

Thus, when the telescope is in normal adjustment,

$$\text{Magnifying power} = \frac{\text{Focal length of objective}}{\text{Focal length of eyepiece}}.$$

Resolving power of a telescope.

We have seen that, in order to produce a high magnifying power, a telescope must have an objective of long focal length, and an eyepiece of short focal length. The Yerkes telescope, having an objective of focal length 62 ft. and eyepiece of focal length $\frac{1}{4}$ in., produces a magnifying power of about 3000. It would be possible to double this magnifying power by making a telescope twice as long with an objective of focal length 124 ft. No real advantage, however, would be gained by so doing. For although the size of the image would be doubled, *no further detail would be made visible.* It would be like stretching an india-rubber sheet on which a picture was painted. The picture would become larger but not more detailed.

The ability of a telescope to show detail in the image is called its *resolving power*, and depends on the aperture of the objective—the wider the aperture the higher the resolving power.

Fig. 138

It can be shown, on the wave theory of light, that the image of a bright point formed by a lens is a bright spot surrounded by dark rings, as shown very much magnified in Fig. 138. Two neighbouring points can just be distinguished if the central bright spot in the image of the one lies on the innermost dark ring of the other. Now the rings decrease in diameter as the aperture of the lens is increased. Hence two points which are too close to be distinguished with a small aperture may be resolved if the aperture is increased.

A good illustration of resolving power is the fact that the two headlights of a distant motor-car, at night, appear to be only one light. The diameter of the pupil of the eye is not large enough to enable them to be resolved. A pair of field glasses might resolve them since the aperture of its objectives is much greater than that of the pupil. As the motor-car approaches the angle subtended at the eye by the two headlights increases, and there comes a time when the unaided eye can just resolve them.

The aperture of the objective of the Yerkes telescope is 40 in. This is about the limit that can be attained with a refracting telescope since a large lens would sag under its own weight, being supported only by the edge. Hence the largest telescopes in the world are reflecting telescopes, having a concave mirror as objective. The reflecting telescope at Mount Wilson, California, has an aperture of 100 in. and can resolve double stars $\frac{1}{20}$ sec. of arc apart. It has added so much to our knowledge of stars that a 200 in. reflector is now being constructed.

Reflecting telescopes.

A reflecting telescope has a concave mirror as objective which forms a real image. This real image is magnified by a converging eyepiece, acting as an ordinary magnifying glass. In order that the observer may not get "in his own light" the rays from the concave objective are reflected to the side, in the Newtonian form of reflecting telescope, by means of a plane mirror (see Fig. 139). The real image is shifted by the plane mirror from I'_1 to I_1. The position of the foot of the image I_1 is obtained by imagining a ray along the axis, after being reflected back along its own path by the concave mirror, to be reflected at the plane mirror (see line marked ·······.) The eyepiece forms a magnified virtual image of I_1, but this final image is not shown in Fig. 139.

Instead of a plane mirror, small convex or concave mirrors are sometimes used. There are several different arrangements for reflecting light to the eyepiece.

The 100 *in. reflector at Mount Wilson.*

In the 100 in. reflector at Mount Wilson (see Fig. 140) there are several possible optical arrangements. When the telescope is used in the Newtonian form, light from the concave objective is reflected to the side at a small plane mirror near the upper end of the telescope tube, where a platform is provided for the observer. When used in the Cassegrain form, light is reflected from the concave objective to a small convex mirror and then back to a plane mirror which directs the light to the side near the lower end of the telescope tube, giving the objective an effective focal length of 250 ft. (see Fig. 141).

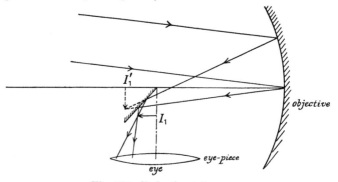

Fig. 139. Reflecting telescope.

Mount Wilson is one of the peaks in the Sierra Madre range, California, over 5000 ft. above sea-level. Here, observations are possible for 290 days in the year. The observatory was erected in 1904, mainly for solar research. At first a 60 in. reflector was used, but in 1906 Mr John D. Hooker made a gift of $45,000 to pay for a 100 in. mirror. A rough disc of glass was cast in France and in 1910 grinding was begun. After six years of work the mirror was finished. It is a paraboloid, 101 in. in diameter, 13 in. thick, and weighs 4½ tons. It is re-silvered twice yearly (see Fig. 142).

Owing to its large aperture it renders stars 250,000 times brighter than they appear with the naked eye, and with its aid many stars may be seen which are too dim to be seen with smaller telescopes.

Fig. 140. The 100 in. reflecting telescope at Mount Wilson. The telescope tube is supported by a rectangular steel yoke, the drums at the ends. of which float in mercury. Light travels down the tube to the concave mirror, 100 in. in diameter, at the bottom, and is reflected up the tube again. It is reflected to an eyepiece, near the top, at the side, by a plane mirror. The observer mounts a high movable platform—not shown in the picture. Alternatively, in the Cassegrain form, the light is reflected at the concave mirror to a convex mirror at the top and down the tube again to a plane mirror which reflects the light to an eyepiece at the side (see Fig. 141).

A telescope has to be mounted in such a way that it can move steadily and "follow" the star it is being used to observe. Otherwise the star would pass rapidly out of the field of view owing to the rotation of the earth. The telescope is made to rotate about the "polar axis", an axis parallel to the axis of rotation of the earth, in the opposite direction to that of the rotation of the earth, so that its direction may remain fixed in space. It can be moved at right angles to the polar axis in order to observe points at various heights in the sky.

The 100 in. reflecting telescope at Mount Wilson weighs 100 tons. It is held in a rectangular steel yoke (see Fig. 140) which is the polar axis. It can be moved with great ease and precision by powerful driving clocks.

History of telescopes.

There are conflicting claims as to who invented the telescope, but it seems probable that the first instrument, an astronomical telescope, was made by a Dutch spectacle maker, Hans Lippershey, about the year 1608. It is said that one day, while holding a lens in either hand, he was astonished on looking through them both together to find that they caused the weathervane on a distant steeple to appear nearer.

In 1609 Galileo made a telescope with a diverging eyepiece. He had, no doubt, seen or heard of the Dutch instrument, but to him belongs the credit of realising how potent an instrument of research the telescope could be. It was, indeed, an epoch-making invention. With its aid, Galileo made a number of astronomical discoveries of immense significance. He discovered that the moon had mountains and valleys and was a world like the earth. He found that Jupiter had moons which revolved round him, that Venus underwent phases like the moon, and that there were spots on the sun which moved, indicating that the sun was rotating. These discoveries convinced Galileo of the truth of the Copernican theory, that the earth revolves round the sun. For supporting this theory he was persecuted by the Inquisition. Galileo made telescopes of magnifying powers of 3, 8 and 33 diameters. He had to grind all his own lenses.

After Galileo, Huygens, the propounder of the wave theory, made an improved telescope, and discovered the nature of Saturn's rings.

Fig. 141. An observer using the 100 in. reflector at Mount Wilson in the Cassegrain form (see also Fig. 140).

In 1761 Sir Isaac Newton made a reflecting telescope with a magnifying power of 38 diameters, a very fine instrument for that time. He made the mirror of speculum, a bright alloy of copper and tin. Gregory had earlier designed a reflecting telescope, but did not possess the mechanical skill to construct it.

By courtesy of the Mount Wilson Observatory

Fig. 142. The 100 in. mirror in the silvering room, where it is re-silvered twice yearly. It is silvered on the front to avoid multiple images.

In 1783 William Herschel, one of the greatest astronomers of all time, made a reflecting telescope with a concave mirror objective of 20 ft. focal length, and in 1789 he succeeded in constructing a much larger one, having an objective of 40 ft. focal length and 4 ft. aperture. The shaping and polishing of so large a mirror was a wonderful achievement. With the aid of this telescope, Herschel mapped out the whole of the sky of the northern hemisphere. One of his great discoveries was the planet Uranus.

The work of John Dollond (died 1761) and Joseph Fraunhofer (1787–1826) on achromatism and the manufacture and shaping of optical glass laid the foundations for modern refracting telescopes.

A very large reflecting telescope was built in Ireland by Lord Rosse, and completed in 1845. The aperture of the objective was 6 ft. and its focal length about 58 ft.

By courtesy of the Mount Wilson Observatory

Fig. 143. The dome of the 100 in. reflector showing the shutter open. Note the shrubs planted there which absorb the sun's rays. If the mountain were subjected to the glare of direct sunlight, convection currents would be set up in the air making accurate observations impossible.

There was no further advance in the size of telescopes until the twentieth century. Several large telescopes have been made in the last thirty years, not appreciably larger than that of Lord Rosse, but optically much more perfect. The largest of them, the 100 in. telescope at Mount Wilson, has already been described.

Experiments.

The student should set up for himself a simple example of each type of telescope described in this chapter.

For example, to set up an astronomical telescope, obtain two converging lenses, one of long and one of short focal length. Find their focal lengths approximately by focusing the image of a distant window on to a sheet of paper with each lens, and measuring the distance of the paper from the lens. Hence calculate the expected magnifying power, *F*. Set up the lenses so that they are separated by a distance equal to their combined focal lengths. Estimate the magnifying power produced by looking through the telescope with one eye, and direct at the object viewed, with the other.

SUMMARY

The simple microscope consists of a converging lens and the compound microscope of two converging lenses, both of short focal length.

All refracting telescopes possess a converging lens as objective which forms a real image. This image is viewed by a magnifying eyepiece, a converging lens in the case of an astronomical telescope and a diverging lens in the case of a Galilean telescope. Reflecting telescopes possess a concave mirror as objective which forms a real image, magnified by a converging eyepiece.

The magnifying power of a telescope

$$= \frac{\text{Apparent size of image}}{\text{Apparent size of object}}$$

$$= \frac{\text{Angle subtended at eye by image}}{\text{Angle subtended at eye by object}}.$$

QUESTIONS

1. Explain, with a diagram, how a simple magnifying glass works. A circular hole $\frac{1}{10}$ in. in radius is viewed by a magnifying glass of 1 in. focal length held at a distance of $\frac{1}{2}$ in. from the hole. What will be the apparent size of the hole as viewed through the glass?

(O. & C.)

2. Describe how you would arrange two lenses to form a microscope. Illustrate your answer by drawing a diagram to show the path of the rays by which an eye sees an image of an object not on the axis through the microscope.   (O. & C.)

3. Describe, with a diagram, an astronomical telescope, indicating the nature and relative focal lengths of the lenses used, their relative positions, and the nature and positions of the images formed.

What would be the effect on the brightness of the image of doubling the diameter of the objective? What would be the effect on the magnifying power of doubling the focal length of the objective and halving the focal length of the eyepiece?   (O. & C.)

4. Describe the arrangement of a converging and a diverging lens to form a telescope, and draw the path of a pencil of light from a point not on the axis to the eye of the observer.   (O. & C.)

5. Explain, with a diagram, the construction of a pair of prism binoculars. Upon what factors does the magnifying power of the binoculars depend?   (O. & C.)

6. How would you arrange two convex lenses of focal lengths 5 cm. and 15 cm. respectively so as to form a simple telescope? Draw the course of a pencil of rays through the instrument and show how to calculate the magnifying power when it is focused for infinity.

(O. & C.)

7. If the distance of the moon from the earth is 240,000 miles and its diameter is 2000 miles, what will be the diameter of the real image of the moon formed by a telescope objective of focal length 60 ft.?

(O. & C.)

8. A microscope consists of an objective and eyepiece of focal lengths 1 cm. and 2 cm. respectively. An object is placed 1·1 cm. from the objective. Find the distance between the objective and eyepiece if the final image is seen at a distance of 25 cm. from the eye.

(C.)

9. A compound microscope is made up of two thin convex lenses each of focal length 1 in. The final image seen by the eye is formed 10 in. from the eyepiece. Find the distance of the object from the objective if the lenses are 8 in. apart.

Sketch the path through the instrument of a narrow pencil of light from a point on the object not on the axis to the eye. (C.)

10. A microscope consists of an objective of focal length 1 cm. and an eyepiece of focal length 4 cm., the distance between the centres of the lenses being 14·5 cm. An object of height 1 mm. is placed 1·1 cm. from the objective. Calculate the position and size of the image seen through the microscope. (C.)

11. Explain fully the following terms when used in connection with telescopes: (a) apparent size, (b) magnifying power, (c) normal adjustment, (d) resolving power.

12. Trace a pair of rays through a terrestrial telescope. Distinguish carefully between any construction lines you require to draw and the rays.

13. Describe, with the aid of a diagram, a simple type of reflecting telescope. What are its advantages and disadvantages as compared with a refracting telescope?

14. The objective of the astronomical telescope at the Lick Observatory has a focal length of 1500 cm. What must be the focal length of the eyepieces to give a magnifying power of (a) 300, (b) 500?

15. A simple astronomical telescope has an objective of focal length 100 cm. and an eyepiece of focal length 5 cm. Find the magnifying power when the instrument is used to view a distant object if the final image is formed (a) at a great distance, (b) at a distance of 25 cm., from the eyepiece.

Draw ray diagrams for the two cases and calculate in each case the distance between objective and eyepiece.

16. Fig. 144 represents a camera viewfinder. F_1 and F_2 are the principal foci of the objective O and eyepiece E respectively. Trace rays from a distant object and show in your diagram the positions

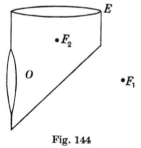

Fig. 144

of the images formed. (The inclined line represents a mirror.)

ANSWERS TO QUESTIONS

CHAPTER III (page 53)

2. 0·26 cm.
6. 77,500 m.p.sec.
8. 9 cm., 1·5.
10. 1·74.
16. 38° 30'.
17. (a) 58°, (b) 60°.
19. 1·532.

CHAPTER IV (page 74)

1. (a) 3 in. beyond; 1·2 in.; real, inverted, magnified.
   (b) 4 in. in front; 3·0 in.; virtual, erect, magnified.
2. $3\frac{1}{4}$ cm. in front; 1 cm.; virtual, erect, diminished.
5. $22\frac{2}{9}$ cm., $\frac{1}{9}$th size.
6. Diverging, $-4\frac{2}{7}$ in.
7. $11\frac{1}{11}$ in.
8. $3\frac{3}{23}$, $3\frac{1}{13}$, $3\frac{3}{110}$, $3\frac{1}{133}$, 3 in., from plate.
9. 80 cm. from candle, 16 cm.
10. $18\frac{3}{4}$ cm., 25 cm. from screen, $\frac{1}{3}$ size of object.
11. $26\frac{2}{3}$ cm., $13\frac{1}{3}$ cm.
12. $3\frac{1}{3}$ in. from object.
16. 8 ft. $11\frac{9}{7}$ in. from lens.
18. Converging, 50 cm. from object, $47\frac{1}{2}$ cm.
19. 12 cm.
20. $8\cdot70 \times 10^5$ miles.
21. 1 in.
22. $19\frac{10}{14}$ cm.
23. 1·37 ($1\frac{4}{11}$).
24. 0·31 in.
27. Between the lenses, $\frac{3}{4}$ cm. from the diverging lens; $\frac{3}{4}$ cm. high.
28. $\frac{2}{3}$ in. beyond the second lens; 0·53 in. high.

CHAPTER V (page 92)

6. Converging, 2 dioptres.
7. Diverging, $-1\frac{1}{3}$ dioptres.
9. -40 in., $5\frac{5}{7}$ in.
10. $2\frac{4}{7}$ dioptres.
11. $2\frac{1}{3}$ dioptres, -1 dioptre.

CHAPTER VI (page 106)

1. (a) 7·5 cm. in front; 0·75 cm.; real, inverted, diminished.
   (b) 7·5 cm. behind; 3·75 cm.; virtual, erect, magnified.
2. 2·4 cm. behind; 0·8 cm.; virtual, erect, diminished.
5. 30 cm.
6. $26\frac{2}{3}$ cm.
7. 8 in. from mirror.
10. $2\frac{2}{3}$ cm. behind mirror; $1\frac{2}{3}$.
11. 5 in.
12. $15\frac{1}{3}$ cm. in front.
13. $\frac{3}{13}$; $2\frac{4}{13}$ in. behind; virtual, erect, diminished.
14. $1\frac{1}{5}$ in. behind; $1\frac{1}{5}$ in.
19. 30 cm.
20. 1·47.

CHAPTER IX (page 151)

2. 25·9 c.p. **3.** 14·4 c.p. **4.** 2 sec. **5.** 1 : 1·32.
6. $\frac{3}{5}$ ft. from 1 c.p. lamp. **7.** 12 c.p. **8.** 12·5 in. **9.** 17·3 %.
12. 2 ft. candles. **13.** 3·16 ft. **15.** $4\frac{17}{27}$: 1.
16. 24, 13·9, 5·86, 3·00, 1·74, 0·89. **17.** 81.

CHAPTER X (page 173)

7. 6 in. **8.** $12\frac{23}{27}$ cm. **9.** $1\frac{11}{67}$ in.
10. 28 cm. from eyepiece; 8 cm. high.
15. (a) 20, (b) 24.

INDEX

For EU product safety concerns, contact us at Calle de José Abascal, 56–1°,
28003 Madrid, Spain or eugpsr@cambridge.org.

www.ingramcontent.com/pod-product-compliance
Ingram Content Group UK Ltd.
Pitfield, Milton Keynes, MK11 3LW, UK
UKHW020308140625
459647UK00014B/1790